The Mini-Mystic Se

BECOMING WHOLE

by Jessica Onsaga

This series is dedicated to the sons of God who will say "YES" to Yahweh no matter the cost. May these books help you grow in sonship and maturity in your walk with Christ.

The Mini-Mystic Series: BEcoming Whole
Jessica Onsaga

Copyright © 2023

Published by Seraph Creative
ISBN 978-1-958997-26-0

www.seraphcreative.org

TABLE OF CONTENTS

Foreword   6

Introduction   12

Chapter 1: Starting The Journey   14

Chapter 2: Perfect Love Casts Out Fear   26

Chapter 3: Rejected or Accepted?   42

Chapter 4: I Will Never Leave You   50

Chapter 5: The Gift of Forgiveness   58

Chapter 6: The Way Out of Sadness   74

Chapter 7: Insecure to Secure   98

Chapter 8: #Triggered   106

Chapter 9: Overcoming Exhaustion   112

Chapter 10: Walking Out Wholeness   122

FOREWORD

What an honor to contribute a humble forward to Jessica Onsaga's wonderful guide into a fuller, deeper relationship with our loving and gracious Heavenly Father. This book, together with its two precedents, provides a Holy Spirit anointed map to "growing and increasing in God's grace and intimacy with our Lord and Savior, Jesus Christ" (2 Peter 3:18). Now having pastored for over 40 years, it is extremely gratifying to see a new generation of Dread Champions being raised up to lead their generation in what I believe to be the Great and Final Harvest of souls and the transition of the ages from the Church Age into the Age of the Eternal Kingdom!

I know Jessica well and had the joy of watching her grow through the stages of maturity from her infancy into the beautiful, wise, and charactered woman that she is today. Apart from Jesus and her dear parents, no one could be prouder. Both Jessica and her wonderful husband Gonzo were a part of our ministry team for years at *The Church of Glad Tidings* here in Yuba City, California. As a young, newlywed couple, they served in ministry through some of the most difficult and trying challenges imaginable – and always with courage, faith, integrity, and exemplary Christian character. I respect them highly and am thrilled to see Jessica guiding others on the path that I have seen her walk herself. Jessica is not a theoretician! What she shares comes from her heart and her own experience and will be life-changing for anyone who "has an ear to hear" what Holy Spirit is saying through her writings. I have now pastored hundreds of young couples, but none that I have more confidence in than Jessica and Gonzo!

So much for the author – but what about the book itself?

One hundred and ninety-three times in Scripture, the Almighty God is called our "Father," and we humans are repeatedly referred to as His "Family" (e.g. Ephesians 1:5), His "children" (e.g. Matthew 5:9) and His "sons & daughters" (e.g. 2 Corinthians 6:18). Although we often take it for granted, it seems to be *a really big deal* to Him! What is so important about this "divine sonship" thing? Couldn't He just as easily have arranged for those who trusted Him for the forgiveness of their sins to just go to Heaven when they died, escape judgment, and live happily ever after? Of course He could have, but – as the old saying goes – Father knows best! A careful consideration of the economy of man's redemption shows us that God both created us in His likeness and image, and that *He is allowing us a maturing process to become like Him in character and nature!* Getting us to Heaven is NOT the big event! Seeing us grow into maturity *in this life* is what He is after! Let's look deeply into the rich truths of these key verses and see what the Holy Spirit may quicken to us about "*BEcoming Whole*" as God's sons and daughters.

"As long as an heir is a child, he is no better off than a slave, even though he owns everything. He is placed under the control of guardians and trustees until the time set by his father" (Galatians 4:1-2).

- If being a child of God is the "end all" of our salvation experience, why would this verse imply that being a child is no better than being a slave?

- Have you considered that your immaturity may be the cause of you "being no better off than a slave"?

- How does this truth apply to you in your spiritual maturity?

"All creation is waiting eagerly for that future day when **God will reveal who His children really are**. Against its will, all creation was subjected to God's curse. But **with eager hope, the creation looks forward to the day when it will join God's children in glorious freedom from death and decay**. For we know that all creation has been groaning as in the pains of childbirth right up to the present time. And we believers also groan, even though we have the Holy Spirit within us as a foretaste of future glory, for we long for our bodies to be released from sin and suffering. **We, too, wait with eager hope for the day when God will give us our full rights as his adopted children…**" (Romans 8:19-23).

- What might the future revelation of God's true children reveal to creation?

- Have you ever considered that "all of creation" is waiting for us to mature as God's sons and daughters?

- What might be implied by us receiving our "full rights" as God's adopted children?

"Now these are the gifts Christ gave to the church: the apostles, the prophets, the evangelists, and the pastors and teachers. Their responsibility is to equip God's people to do His work and build up the church, the body of Christ. This will continue until we all come to such unity in our faith and knowledge of God's Son that **we will be mature in the Lord, measuring up to the full and complete standard of Christ. Then we will no longer be immature like children.** We won't be **tossed and blown about** by every wind of new teaching. We will not be influenced when people try to trick us with lies so clever they sound like the truth. Instead, we will speak the truth in love, **growing in every way more and more like Christ**, who is the head of his body, the church" (Ephesians 4:11-15).

- Have you ever considered the possibility of "measuring up to the full and complete standard of Christ" in your life?

- Have you ever considered that the storms of life that "toss and blow you about" may be related to your immaturity as a son/daughter of God?

- What do your "chalk marks" on the wall tell you about your spiritual growth rate over the past ten years of your life?

"As many as received Him (Christ Jesus), to them **He gave power to become the sons of God,** even to all that believe on His name: which were born, not of blood, nor of the will of the flesh, nor of the will of man, but of the will of God" (John 1:12-13).

- Have you mused over the fact that when we receive Christ, He **empowers us to become** sons of God?

- What's the difference between being "born again" and being empowered to become a "son" of God?

There are many reasons that believers in the "Western Tradition" of Christianity have little understanding of these important truths, but we should consider three:

1. First of all, we have a "great adversary" (Satan) who has worked diligently to keep us from understanding the incredible significance and worth of Divine Sonship! He knows it will cause him a bruised head if God's kids ever truly understand their rights as God's mature sons and daughters.

2. Secondly, the Great American Enterprise in the West has focused almost exclusively on making it into heaven, instead of the great and precious promises available to us in _this_ life! Western Christianity has focused on "pie in the sky by and by" while authentic biblical Christianity's main focus is "steak on your plate while you wait!"

3. Lastly, we read Scripture through the distorted lens of our "approximate" English language, instead of the "articulate" Greek language that the New Testament was written in. Because of that, we view being born again, being a child of God, and being a son of God as being roughly synonymous, when in fact they are quite different in the language of Scripture, employing distinct terms for an infant in the womb (brephos), a toddler (nepios), a student (teknon) and a fully mature son (huios)! This language confusion has stolen from us the importance of what is perhaps the primary focus of our redemption: A chance to be transformed, in this life, into the fullness of the image of our "Big Brother" – Jesus Christ!

With this enlightened understanding of Scripture, fantastic new horizons open up before us! Instead of the confused muddle of approximate English meanings, we suddenly see a glorious calling to become fully mature (huios) sons and daughters who are qualified heirs of their Father's kingdom, and joint heirs ("equal participants") with Christ Jesus!

And this is what Jessica's wonderful series will lead you into! Having laid a firm foundation in her previous two volumes, here she will take you step by step through the necessary processes of **BEcoming Whole** and of discovering the beauty of knowing better and walking closer to your precious Heavenly Father (whose will for you will always exceed your most unbelievable dreams and your wildest imaginations)!

> "Never doubt God's mighty power to work in you and accomplish all this. He will achieve infinitely more than your greatest request, your most unbelievable dream, and exceed your wildest imagination! He will outdo them all, for His miraculous power constantly energizes you" (Ephesians 3:20).

Pastor Dave Bryan;
Church of Glad Tidings, Yuba City, California; USA

INTRODUCTION

This is the third book of The Mini-Mystic Series. The series was written to help believers grow and mature in their walk with Yahweh! The first book, The Foundation, lays the theological base on which all other books are written. So, it is important and helpful to read The Foundation first. If you don't start with the first book, you may not understand the framework on which all the books in the series are built. The other books in the series can be read in any order, but the tools taught in The Foundation are especially important for receiving what this book carries.

The Mini-Mystic Series is intended to help you start a conversation with Yahweh and go deeper into Him. I won't quote every verse or fully explain every topic I write about. That is intentional. My hope is that you search out the things I share so that you can discover them for yourself. The goal is that you bring everything you learn and read in this book to Jesus. He will sift them and show you how this information can equip you in your personal journey with Him. These words will only become more head knowledge if you do not allow Jesus to show you the heart revelation in them. Head knowledge is anything you have learned *about* Jesus but doesn't truly know or believe in your heart (soul). Head knowledge is dangerous because it inoculates people against the truth. They think they *know* the truth, but they don't know Truth Himself. True transformation happens as we encounter and agree with Truth in our soul. This is why learning to abide in Jesus is vital for sons of God to mature and grow. The Mini-mystic series is set up to give you just enough information to make you hungry for more. I want you to go and seek Jesus about everything that is said in these books. As we seek Him, we become more like Him.

In Growing in Sonship (Book 2), we covered wrong belief systems. In this book, we will cover soul wounds to help us go deeper in our journey of maturing as sons. Part of growing in sonship is renewing the mind, which includes facing our deepest soul wounds. Our soul wounds and the lies we believe play a major role in holding us back from walking in the fullness and abundant life that Jesus has for us. As we face our past, we receive our inheritance. This book will be challenging, but so freeing if you are willing to face the dark places of your soul and bring them to Jesus. Inner healing isn't easy, but in my opinion, it is always worth the pain. Once the pain is brought to Jesus, we can then start the healing journey to be free of it forever! Healing is a beautiful part of our journey, and if we embrace the process, we will find that God is better and more faithful than we previously knew. If you are ready for more, then buckle up! We are in for a ride.

Chapter One

STARTING THE JOURNEY

I was a broken, lost, and religious Christian. All my head knowledge (from reading the Bible, teachings, and books) was not enough to heal the pain my soul was in. Religion didn't help me with my soul wounds. I could even say that religion REINFORCED some of my soul wounds. Jesus is the ONLY source of life and healing. Religious duties and teachings don't have ANY ability to heal a soul. As we begin to have a personal relationship with Jesus and RECEIVE His healing, our soul begins the journey of transformation. I do want to note that even in a personal relationship with Jesus, it is possible to hear the truth and spend time with Jesus, and yet still choose to remain unhealed.

> James 1:22 (TPT) "Don't just listen to the Word of Truth and not respond to it, for that is the essence of self-deception. So always let his Word become like poetry written and fulfilled by your life!"

The key to renewing the mind (soul transformation) is our agreement with truth. Reading the truth in the Bible, hearing the truth from a sermon, or even talking to Jesus Himself won't transform us unless we RECEIVE the truth into our hearts. Judas walked with Jesus in the flesh for years! However, because his heart didn't receive the truth he was hearing, he remained deceived. This proves that it is not about our knowledge of truth or even having a personal relationship with Jesus. Soul transformation comes down to our RECEPTION of what Jesus says.

My journey of healing started at a youth group winter camp. I was very religious, but my soul was tormented by fear and pain. At that camp, I heard about having a personal and close relationship with Jesus instead of a distant slave relationship with God. In my first personal interaction (encounter) with Yahweh, I saw myself in torn and stained clothes. I approached a peaceful cabin that was surrounded by a beautiful garden. As I opened the little gate leading to the cabin, Father God ran off the porch towards me in overwhelming love. He met me on the path leading to the front door, but I couldn't face Him. Father God was so excited to see me that He wanted to lift me up and engulf me in a giant hug. In spite of His excitement, He restrained Himself for my sake because I was not ready for that. Trembling with shame and insecurity, I looked down at the ground as I said, "They told me you loved me." Father God gently lifted my chin. I was so confused as I watched the vision play out. I scoffed and thought to myself, "*Duh, I know He loves me. And I am not insecure and broken like that.*" I was "strong", not weak like this vision portrayed. Even though I didn't understand what I was seeing, I stayed engaged in the encounter to see what else would happen. As Father God lifted my chin, His eyes of love pierced my soul. Every wound was seen, and my past was exposed, but despite the hot mess my soul was in, I was still deeply loved by Him. He fully saw me, and He cherished me for me. I don't know how to explain the depth and power of what Father God told me at that moment. His words were more than just words... they were LIFE itself. They pierced through my heart and awoke something inside me, "I have always loved you, truly loved you for you. I have been waiting for this moment. Welcome home." The moment He spoke to my heart, I was wrecked. The vision was done, and I was undone.

That first encounter changed my life forever. If I had stopped the encounter or rejected it because I didn't understand it, I would have missed this pivotal moment in my life. I wasn't instantly healed at camp. My fears weren't all gone, and neither were my soul wounds all healed in that first encounter. BUT it was the beginning of my journey into wholeness. I chose to receive the words that Yahweh and Jesus said to me, and I began to see my soul radically change. The blinders were gradually coming off, and I began walking in more peace and joy than ever before. This freedom is what I want to share with everyone, and it is the reason for writing this series.

Facing my soul wounds was incredibly hard. My darkest fears, pains, and emotions were locked away... deep, DEEP in my heart. I didn't *want* to face the darkest areas of my soul. I had worked very hard to keep them locked away, so I DIDN'T have to face them. Jesus showed me that the longer I stuffed my soul wounds, the more energy it would take to keep them locked up... AND that eventually, the pain would outgrow my ability to keep them locked up. It was already affecting my life, but I couldn't see it. I was coping with my soul wounds and was so busy that I didn't notice.

Jesus kept inviting me deeper into His heart. I was so hungry for more of Jesus, but as I grew closer to Him, my soul wounds kept coming up and were resistant to Jesus. That is when it really began to become clear... to have more of Jesus, I would have to face the darkness in my soul. It was like a heavy weight that was preventing me from flying with Jesus. I chose to trust Him. I decided that all I wanted was Jesus, no matter the cost. I felt like I was risking everything to face the pain monsters in my soul. And to my surprise, Jesus was big enough for everything that I faced! I thought I would have to "die and go to Heaven" to be free from all my soul pain... and I was so wrong! I had such a small view of Jesus when I was in religion.

The biggest stumbling blocks to our growth as sons of God are wrong beliefs and soul wounds. Every belief and soul wound influences how we perceive reality and affects our relationship with Yahweh. Most of the time, we are blinded to how much havoc our soul wounds cause in our lives. When I started my inner healing journey, I was SO broken, blind, and lost... even though I had been a Christian my whole life. I couldn't see how fear, anger, and many soul wounds were affecting EVERY area of my life. The more I healed, the hungrier I became for more healing. I didn't know I could feel so good! I began to see that I was blinded by my dysfunction.

My abundant life reality was being filtered out by my wrong beliefs and soul wounds to the point that all I could think about was myself...

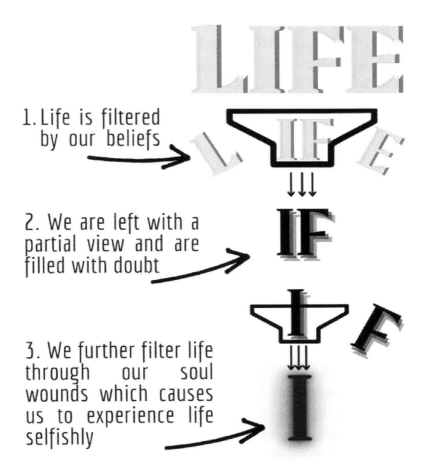

1. Life is filtered by our beliefs

2. We are left with a partial view and are filled with doubt

3. We further filter life through our soul wounds which causes us to experience life selfishly

Abundant life is ALREADY our current reality... we are just blinded to it. The more our soul wounds heal and the more we believe the truth, the more we will see and live in abundant life. We are the ones filtering all that God has given us. The good news is that Jesus has done ALL the work for our salvation, healing, and breakthrough. All we have to do is receive what He has already done.

When we get to the root of our soul pain, we see that it is just an indicator pointing to an area of our soul that hasn't agreed with Truth... YET. A dear friend of mine had a vision about the reality of our pain and soul wounds. In the vision, she was walking with Jesus in the garden of her heart. She looked around and saw the many soul wounds that her heart was carrying. To her shock though, the soul wounds were these egg-shaped objects that sat ON TOP of the garden ground. Her heart wasn't actually wounded... she WAS healed. And although the wounds *were* present, they weren't affecting her healing. What Jesus had done couldn't be undone. He had healed her, and she could choose to agree with the healing she already received, or she could choose to allow the wounds to reside in her heart. The choice was hers.

I believe all inner healing can be summed up by this: **Any area of our soul where we agree with or choose something OTHER than Jesus is an area that causes death in our life. To be healed of our soul wounds, all we need to do is choose Jesus and His truth instead of the pain and its lies.** It's very simple, yet incredibly hard to walk out. All we have to do is say, "Yes" to Jesus in every area of our soul and everything would be healed, but choosing Jesus over our soul pain is a very intense process. Every fear, rejection, offense, trauma, and life experience has told us one thing, but Jesus says another. Allowing Jesus to re-teach us everything we thought we knew is hard, but it is absolutely worth the work! Thankfully, it does get easier and easier over time as our soul begins to trust Jesus more.

I am not trying to make light of the most intense and painful areas of our souls. My intention is to break down our emotional stumbling blocks into tangible, bite-size pieces so we can see BEHIND the walls of pain. When all we see is our pain, we lose sight of Jesus. If we can step back from the soul wounds and see what's really going on, it will help our soul cling to Jesus instead of the pain. So, in this book, we will systematically address and break down some of the most common soul wounds that everyone faces.

Each moment we decide (usually subconsciously) who or what we are going to agree with. Yahweh's truth is eternally resounding through all of creation, but the enemy accuses Yahweh with twisted lies and distorted truth. Even demonic oppression boils down to our soul agreeing with a lie from the enemy. We either agree with the demon or Jesus. "The devil made me do it" is a lie from the enemy trying to make us believe that we are powerless. There is no force or spirit in all of creation strong enough to take away our gift of free will. If the enemy was able to... then we would ALL be dead.

> *John 10:10 (BSB) "The thief comes only that he might steal and might kill and might destroy. I came that they may have life, and have it in all its fullness."*

Every soul wound is an area of our hearts where we have bought into a lie. Whatever we agree with has influence and authority in our lives. Just because we bought into a lie, does NOT mean we are eternally locked into that choice. At any moment, we can choose to reject the lie and receive truth in its place. This process is what the Bible refers to as: renewing the mind. The more we agree with Truth, the more our soul and life transform. To start the journey of soul transformation, there are a few things to keep in mind:

- *Feelings* **are not indicators of truth**. The enemy doesn't lie to us about obscure things. That would be too obvious, and we probably wouldn't bite. What the enemy does is take *part* of what's true and weave a lie into it. So, it *feels* true to us... because it is partly true. The more we agree with the enemy's lies, the more deceived and unsound we become. *(An unsound state of mind is any area of our mind that doesn't carry the sound/frequency of Heaven.)* Usually, what Jesus says to us will actually *feel* wrong at first because we are blinded and deceived. Truth feels and sounds like a lie to an unsound mind. This is why our feelings are not indicators of truth. When we choose to start believing Jesus instead of the lie, it is a CHOICE, not a feeling.

You can compare inner healing to changing a habit our physical body has. Take a moment and cross your arms. Now cross your arms the opposite way (For example, right over left, then vice versa). If you actually did try folding your arms one way and then another (instead of just reading this), then you would feel/understand that one way *feels* normal or right, and the other *feels* awkward or wrong. The awkwardness we feel when we cross our arms or interlock our fingers a different way illustrates how awkward the truth can *feel* to our souls. Our soul has only known one way of living (in lies and brokenness). So, when we begin to walk in a new way of living (in truth and wholeness), it *feels* awkward and wrong to our soul while it is in process.

- **Healing soul wounds will take TIME, and the amount of time it takes to be healed depends on the level of surrender and diligence in which we approach the soul wound.** Healing soul wounds can be explained in a similar way to how we correct bad habits. Our soul has a habit of carrying the pain and agreeing with the lie. It will take time for our soul to learn a new habit of agreeing with truth instead of the lie. If we are uncompromising with our rejection of the lie and reception of the truth, then our soul wound will be healed quicker. If we aren't fully surrendered in addressing the soul wound and diligent in choosing the truth, the healing takes longer.

- It's not about what happens to us; it is all about how we PERCEIVE events around us. An event that may be a BIG deal to one person, may not even be noticed by someone else (like having to rearrange your day because of an unexpected circumstance). WE decide how we perceive and process life around us. It is possible to go through this life without taking on any lies from the enemy in spite of what happens to us. Jesus experienced rejection, betrayal, and all sorts of brokenness in this world, and yet He never partnered with any lies of the enemy. Jesus showed us what was possible for us — that we could live in abundant life and wholeness regardless of our circumstances! YAY God!!!

- To be whole, EVERYTHING needs to be brought to Jesus. If our heart is in agreement with lies, then in those areas, we are choosing to partner with death instead of life. Furthermore, all we have known is life WITH our soul wounds and dysfunction, so we are usually blind to the lies of the enemy. We may think we are "doing pretty good", but in reality, we have just become accustomed to our bondage. This is why we want Jesus to sift and heal EVERY area of our life... the good and the bad. As we bring everything to Him, every area of our life begins to be transformed by Life.

- No matter how BIG the soul wounds, Yahweh is always big enough to heal every area of our hearts. The bigger our view of Yahweh is, the more powerful and hopeful we become. His grace is more than enough. His love continually pursues us and invites us out of the pain. The pain can feel overwhelming, especially at the beginning of a healing journey. Our feeling stuck, unhealable, hopeless, and powerless is a LIE from hell trying to keep us bound.

- Celebrate and honor the encounters you do have, no matter how "small" or insignificant they may seem. We are all unique, and our journeys with Yahweh will all be different. It is SO easy to fall into comparison and be frustrated that you don't hear, see, or encounter God like "_____" does. The enemy will make sure that there will ALWAYS be someone you can compare your walk with the Lord to. When our focus is on other people and how they walk with Jesus, then we lose sight of the beautiful things Yahweh is doing in OUR life. Instead, we can focus on our unique and personal relationship with Yahweh and grow it into our own beautiful expression. When we partner with frustration or discouragement over a perceived "lack" in our relationship with Jesus, it stunts our growth and holds us back. It brings death. Celebrating, being grateful for, and honoring where our walk currently is with Jesus will launch us into deeper and more personal encounters. <u>The more we honor what we are given, the more it will grow.</u> The hard part is just REMEMBERING to honor and celebrate the encounters.

If we keep these things in mind while we address our soul wounds, it will help protect our hearts against discouragement and frustration while we are healing. It is very easy to become disheartened when we are facing the painful areas of our soul that we have tried to avoid... BUT we don't have to! We are one with Jesus! We can fix our eyes on Him! The more we fix our eyes on Him, the quicker we heal and the quicker we grow. It naturally becomes less painful because our eyes are on HIM instead of our pain.

Dealing with ANY lie or soul wound can be summed up to these steps:

1. <u>IDENTIFY</u> the lie or soul wound.

    o   For this step, I ask Jesus questions like:

        ▪   What lie am I believing that I am ready to talk about today?

        ▪   Are there any soul wounds that I am ready to be healed of?

2. BREAK AGREEMENT with the lie or soul wound

    o   Once Jesus has identified an area of our soul to
        heal, then it is our choice to agree with what Jesus
        has said or not. This is probably the hardest step.
        As we addressed earlier, deciding to believe Jesus
        beyond our pain and what our soul thinks and feels
        can be very challenging.

    o   For example, once I have identified the lie, I like
        to look directly at the lie or soul wound in the
        encounter. Sometimes the lies or wounds will look
        like beings (nasty creatures, etc.) or objects (chains,
        mud, etc.) Either way, I look at the lie and say
        something like, "I choose to break all agreements
        with you. YOU are a liar and thief, and I no longer
        want you in my life."

3. RECEIVE (or choose to believe) the truth instead of the
    lie

    o   This last step is to receive the truth that Jesus
        showed us regarding our soul wound or lie we were
        believing. To be healed, it is not enough to just reject
        the lies or break agreement with the soul wounds.
        The most important step is to FILL that area of our
        soul with truth... or our soul will return to the lie/
        pain because it doesn't have truth to stand on.

    o   Right after breaking agreement with the lies, I then
        look at Jesus and say something like, "I choose to
        believe what you say, and I will cling to it even if I
        don't understand."

Another way of doing these steps is to do a "trade" with Jesus.
You can give Jesus the lie or soul wound and ask Him what He
will give you in return. He's very good at trading and always
gives truth, a better item, or a feeling (like peace or joy) in
return. Once the trade is complete, it is still important for you
to receive whatever Jesus gave you. It comes down to our

intention. Whether we make a trade with Jesus, break agreement with the lies and choose truth, or use another method, the important thing is that we use our free will to choose Yahweh over anything else.

It would be good to mention that it is impossible to take the knowledge given in this book and heal our souls in our own power. The information does not translate to soul health or maturity. As with Judas, hearing the truth is not merely enough. Our soul was created for connection with Yahweh. This is the singular most important part. SONship is all about oneness and being family WITH Yahweh. Even in inner healing and soul transformation, it is not about us "figuring it out" and muscling ourselves into better shape. EVERYTHING we do and process was meant to be done from intimacy and abiding in Jesus.

In this book, we will explore some of the common soul wounds we all carry and shed some light on the painful areas we keep hidden. At the end of each section, there are self-application prompts to help you in your journey. Please remember these three things when going through the self-applications:

1. The prompts and questions are intended to be processed WITH Jesus over time, not all at once! Remember that it is about the process, not the destination.

2. A fun thing to note is that you can actually revisit previous encounters as often as you like and grow more from them! Those encounters are eternal, which means fresh revelation and wine can come from old encounters as you reengage Yahweh in them!

3. I highly recommend writing down what you heard, felt, saw, or experienced when you asked Jesus the prompt questions. It is very helpful to be able to go back and reread encounters and visions.

With that, we are ready to dive in! It is my honor to share my process with you. I hope that this book becomes a springboard of healing and breakthrough in your life. You already HAVE everything you need within you through your oneness with Jesus. My prayer is that this book and series help you tap into the abundant life that's already in you.

> 2 Peter 1:3-4 (TPT) "Everything we could ever need for life and godliness has already been deposited in us by his divine power. For all this was lavished upon us through the rich experience of knowing him who has called us by name and invited us to come to him through a glorious manifestation of his goodness. As a result of this, he has given you magnificent promises that are beyond all price, so that through the power of these tremendous promises we can experience partnership with the divine nature, by which you have escaped the corrupt desires that are of the world."

> 1 John 2:27 (NLT) "But you have received the Holy Spirit, and he lives within you, so you don't need anyone to teach you what is true. For the Spirit teaches you everything you need to know, and what he teaches is true — it is not a lie. So just as he has taught you, remain in fellowship with Christ."

Chapter Two

PERFECT LOVE CASTS OUT FEAR

Fear is something I was all too familiar with as a child. It was my greatest torment, and now is one of my greatest breakthroughs. I began to partner with fear as a young child after I was sexually abused. To add to it, the abuse opened my spiritual eyes to be able to see the demonic realm. My childhood and early teen years were filled with fear, severe body shame, night terrors, and demonic encounters. From about 6-years-old on, I was tormented by seeing demonic spirits. Thankfully, I usually only saw them at night. I began to hate the night because I had two choices: be tormented by seeing demons while I was awake OR be tormented while I slept by night terrors (intensely bad dreams that felt real). As I grew older, I became more and more afraid of men, afraid of failing, afraid of demonic spirits and night terrors, and afraid of what people thought about me.

Needless to say, I was a broken little girl. All of my religion couldn't touch the deep pain of my soul wounds. I took comfort in the promises I read about in the Bible, but reading the Bible didn't translate into healing in my soul. I knew God loved me, and I knew that perfect love casts out fear... somehow?

This was my life and all that I knew until I was met by Perfect Love. The first night at that youth winter camp is when everything changed. I met Yahweh face-to-face in an encounter for the first time, and it wrecked me in all the right ways. Yahweh wasn't distant or judgmental. In fact, He was very different from almost everything I had been told about Him. I learned that Yahweh saw ME. Yahweh loved ME and wanted a personal relationship with

ME. Yahweh wasn't the distant master I had served my whole life. He was MY loving Father, and He was waiting for me to believe Him over the lies.

After my first encounter, I chose to dive all in. I wanted all of Jesus. His love drew me in, and I chose to receive everything that I could from Yahweh. I gave Him my "YES" and my devotion no matter the cost. Yahweh told me that if I gave Him all of me, that I could have all of Him. Ever since then, I have been on a journey of surrendering every area of my life so that I am truly, fully yielded to Him.

I began to realize that my choice was between receiving Jesus's truth and healing or staying in pain and torment. Instead of staying lost in pain and mad at God, I chose to go TO Him, so I could be made whole. It was incredibly hard to face my deepest fears and soul pain, but I am SO glad I did. Now when I look back at my childhood, all I can see is Jesus covering me during the abuse, and all I feel is His peace and wholeness. It took years of being intentional to bring my pain and fears to Jesus, but it was worth every moment. Fast forward to today, the torment I was in as a child is now a distant memory. The pain, body shame and trauma, the night terrors, and the fears have ALL melted away.

As I walked through the process of choosing truth, I slowly began to see that fear is a liar and a thief. I used to think that the fearful thoughts were helping me stay safe. I couldn't see that fear was my tormentor. It was actively working with all its might to kill, steal, and destroy my life. Fear was my ENEMY! I bought the lie and chose to receive its torment by my own doing. BUT Jesus took everything the enemy meant for evil and used it for my healing and breakthrough. He took all the brokenness and made something beautiful in my heart. I am learning to live in His wholeness in deeper and deeper levels. I definitely don't have it all "figured out" yet (it's not about that anyways!), but I am more free, healthy, and whole than I have ever been. This journey of sonship is a precious and wonderful dance with Jesus. It IS worth the cost.

IMPORTANT NOTE: When talking about fear, it is important to mention that the ONLY fear we are allowed as sons of God is the Fear of the Lord. The Fear of the Lord is the ONLY fear that is NOT a liar or a thief. The Fear of the Lord is not a spirit of fear nor our enemy. According to Isaiah, the Fear of the Lord is one of the seven Spirits of God. The spirit of the Fear of the Lord is pure, holy, and of Yahweh Himself.

Fun note on the Fear of the Lord: It bothered me that Bible translators chose the English word "fear" in the phrase "Fear of the Lord" because Yahweh commands us to NOT fear. So I did some digging and found in Hebrew that the word "fear" in the phrase "Fear of the Lord" is translated from two words, either *pachad* or *yir'âh*.

- *Pachad* is to tremble, to be in trepidation, to be on one's guard, or terror. It IS to be terrified and in dread.

- *Yir'ah* is to reverence, to trust, or to tremble for joy. This root word does not have to do with fear or terror at all. It is a restful confidence and joy!

As I studied these root words and asked Yahweh about them, He showed me something powerful. When we feel *Pachad* (terror or dread), that feeling doesn't come from us. It is the lies and fears that we are in agreement with, and THEY feel terror or dread as Yahweh draws near. God is NOT terrorized or in dread within Himself. Therefore, the Spirit of The Fear of the Lord is not rooted in fear or dread. Since we are one with Christ, this means WE also are not filled with fear or dread towards Yahweh. So, as we address and get free from our agreement with fear, the *pachad* of the Lord we feel turns to *yir'ah* of the Lord! As our soul heals and trusts Yahweh, we begin to feel the reverence, trust, and JOY of the Lord (*yir'ah*). Yahweh explained to me that the Spirit of the Fear of the Lord is always the *yir'ah* in nature, but some people perceive it as *pachad* because of their soul wounds!

So, moving forward, anytime I am talking about fear in this chapter, I am not talking about the Fear of the Lord. I am talking about a spirit of fear that sells us lies. We have covered the nitty-gritty details of fear, and now we can dive into HOW to be free from fear!

NUTS AND BOLTS OF FEAR

Fear:

   a. *a feeling of anxiety or dread*

   b. *a demonic spirit whose character core is fear*

Fear is a core emotion that everyone faces at some point. It is an interesting feeling because every person processes fear differently. What terrifies one person, may be enjoyable to another (like a roller coaster ride). This means fear is subjective and solely depends on the individual. Fear looks different from person to person, and many people are totally blind to areas of fear in their life. Furthermore, anyone can choose to become afraid of anything.

When you break it down, fear starts as a thought or emotion. Not every thought or emotion we *feel* comes from us. The enemy is a thought and emotion suggester. A spirit of fear can suggest a fearful thought or feeling, but it is up to our soul if we will agree with the thought of fear or not. We see examples of this in the garden of Eden when Eve was tempted and again when Jesus was tempted in the desert. Both times, a thought was suggested to them, and it was up to THEM to decide what to do with the thought. Eve chose to agree with the deception. Whereas Jesus tested it against the word of God and rejected Satan's suggestions.

We make these exact same choices EVERY day... most of the time without even realizing it. Moment by moment, our soul (usually subconsciously) decides what to do with every thought and feeling that we come across. Depending on what the soul believes, it chooses to agree with or reject the thoughts that come its way. Our life experiences, what we were told to believe, and our knowledge of the truth, all affect our soul's decisions in what it chooses to agree with.

Fear is talked about again and again because it is SO destructive to our souls. Regardless of how true it *sounds*, fear is a LIAR and a THIEF. It binds us and blinds us to the truth. Fear grips our souls in a way that nothing else does. It affects our physical body... sometimes even to the point of paralyzing us at times. Fear is very tangible and powerful in the way that it affects us. THIS is why "Do not fear" is the most repeated command in the Bible. Fear takes us out of the mind of Christ and replaces it with an unsound mind that cannot think or see clearly.

Fear is the enemy of God; therefore, fear is also our enemy. Furthermore, this enemy HATES you. The spirit of fear is not trying to help you or protect you from harm... instead, fear wants to steal, kill, and destroy our lives. Oftentimes religious people know the command "Do not fear," so they simply change their diction but keep the fear in their hearts. "*I am just concerned.*" "*This is the wise thing to do.*" "*You're being reckless.*" Fear rebranded is still fear and still brings death. Rebranding fear is usually not intentional or a conscious choice. Most of us are unaware that we agree with fear subconsciously. At the end of the day, it doesn't matter that we are unaware... fear is still fear. It IS the enemy and believing its lies will always bring death.

We can choose to be afraid of ANYTHING, which leads to an infinite amount of fear. In the midst of so many fears, all fears can be broken down into a few categories or roots. Pretty much every fear stem from one of these 5 roots:

- Fear of death *(for yourself or someone you love)*

- Fear of pain *(emotional or physical)*

- Fear of failure

- Fear of rejection

- Fear of lack *(there not being enough)*

The FEAR Tree

Fear of calamity · Fear of the unknown · Fear of punishment · Fear of men · Fear of enclosed spaces · Fear of being attacked · Fear of social interactions · Fear of heights · Fear of " " · Fear of bugs · Fear of sickness · Fear of the dark · Fear of God not showing up

Fear of Death · Fear of Failure · Fear of Pain · Fear of Lack · Fear of Rejection

To be free from the infinite branches of the fear tree, these 5 roots need to be challenged against what Jesus says. Each root has a <u>different</u> facet of truth to counter the fear which means that each root needs to be brought to Jesus one at a time. For example, the truth that breaks the fear of death is different from the truth that breaks the fear of failure.

PERFECT LOVE CASTS OUT FEAR

1 John 4:16 (TPT) "We have come into an intimate experience with God's love, and we trust in the love he has for us. God is love!..."

1 John 4:18 (Author's translation) "There is no fear in the Father's agape love, but His perfect

love casts out our fear. For fear conceives torment, and the one who is in torment has not been made whole by the Father's agape love." [inserted agape for clarity. God's love is perfect, whole, and complete. His agape love is perfect love according to the Greek.]

Perfect love is the radical, limitless love of God that pursues us. Agape love is at the core of Yahweh's being and is in everything He does. Though love is not the opposite of fear, it is the only force strong enough to conquer fear. We know this because we can be courageous AND fearful at the same time. For example, a mother may be terrified of a bear, but she can choose courage in spite of the fear to protect her children. Fear and courage can, and often do, coincide within the soul. Courage enables us to function in the midst of fear, but it does not cast it out.

We are made of and held together by Jesus, so it's not just the existence of the perfect love that casts out fear nor is it His infinite power. Perfect Love casts out fear as we begin to choose and receive Yahweh (Perfect Love) in our souls. Seeing truth through the eyes of love AND agreeing with truth is the only way to break the torment of fear. The more we allow agape love to transform us, the more our fears become obsolete.

> *Psalm 23:5 (TPT) "Even when your path takes me through the valley of deepest darkness, fear will never conquer me, for you already have!"*

This is such a POWERFUL version of this verse. *Fear will never conquer me, for you already have!* This is what perfect love casting out fear looks like. Perfect love casts out fear as we agree with and grow in God's love. As this happens, we begin to think and understand the truth, and our fears become unsound.

To be free of all fear, it boils down to this: will you choose to divorce your agreement with each of fear's roots and choose to believe Jesus? Every time you recognize that you are feeling fear is an opportunity to bring that fear to Jesus. When Jesus was tempted, He tested it against the WORD of the Lord. When we bring our fears to Jesus, we are testing them against His WORD. Then we can choose to break agreement with the fear and choose to believe what Jesus says instead. At the beginning of conquering fear, what Jesus says usually doesn't make sense to us... because the fear we agree with causes an unsound mind! When this happens, it comes down to what we choose regardless of our feelings.

I am a rational and logical person. I try to step back and see the big picture. This part of my personality affects how I go about inner healing. Feelings and emotions can be easily manipulated, especially by fear. I can tell a funny story one moment and have people laughing, and then I can tell a sad story the next moment and bring people to tears. Since emotions and feelings can be manipulated, I try to step back and see the root and the big picture. So even if it doesn't *feel* true, I choose what Jesus says over everything else. He has my "yes".

There are different ways to break agreement with the lies of fear and choose what Jesus says instead. Please reference Chapters 5 & 6 of The Foundation for help and troubleshooting blocks when trying to talk to Jesus about fear. Personally, I have found these steps very helpful when addressing and getting free from fear...

1. Recognize the fear(s) and that it was your choice to agree with it. We can only address the things that we are willing to look at.

2. Bring the fear to Jesus and ask what HE says about it. Trying to reject fear is not enough, I must have TRUTH to replace the lie that fear sold me.

3. Choose to break the agreement with the fear and choose to believe whatever Jesus says is true. This is where the rubber meets the road. The lies of fear usually still *sound* true even after hearing the TRUTH. In times like this, I remind myself that Jesus always has my "yes". To reject the lie, I break all agreements with the lie and decide in my heart that the LIE is the enemy. The lie will steal, kill,

and destroy my life so I want nothing to do with it. Even if the truth doesn't *sound* true, I choose to believe it because Jesus is the way, the truth, and the life.

4. STAND FIRM and believe what Jesus says until we are anchored in the truth. Often, I will need to repeat steps 1–3 multiple times. After I reject the lie and choose the truth, I usually don't *feel* a shift in my heart. It takes time for the unsound perspective to become foreign and for the truth to become my new foundation. This is the renewing part of dealing with fear. Dealing with the fear once is not enough to renew your soul's perspective forever. Fear is like an onion. It usually has layers upon layers that our soul believes subconsciously. It may take 100 times of bringing fear to Jesus and choosing the truth. Be patient! Don't lose heart! It doesn't matter how many times it takes. Every time is a step towards truth. Every step towards truth is a step away from partnering with death in our hearts.

These steps are not the only way to deal with fear. There are many ways that Jesus may show you how to strategically deal with the fear you are facing. All you have to do is ask Him. No matter how we go about it, getting free from fear is a process, but it is SO freeing when we do! Fear is the enemy. Fear of failure, fear of pain, or any other fear ALL bring death. We can't see the unsoundness of our fears until we begin to receive Yahweh and His truth. As we choose to believe the Word of Life over the lies of fear, the blinders begin to fall off our eyes. Words can explain this mystery of Perfect Love casting out fear, but only experiencing it will make it understood.

When I was early on in my process of getting free from fear, Yahweh gave me an incredible dream. In the dream, I was in a town ministering when the demon prince of the area decided to make me his next target. The principality manifested himself as a 7ft grizzly bear which meant the beast was even more massive when standing on its hind legs. When I saw the bear, I was instantly seized with fear. I have experienced facing the demonic in the spiritual realm, but seeing it manifest physically terrorized me to the core. Holy Spirit was so close to me the whole time, but I was too afraid to take the time to listen to Him. Despite my attempts to get away, the bear was just too strong and broke through every door and hiding place I found. I tried escaping to the roof of the house, but even that was pointless. When the bear stood on its hind legs, it was able to reach me on top of the house. I jumped off the house and ran for the woods. Obviously, such a massive animal would be able to catch up with me in seconds. Holy Spirit kept telling me over and over that this bear was the principality and that I could take him. Holy Spirit kept challenging me to face the bear and reminded me of the time that God was with King David when he faced the bear. Still running through the forest, I could now feel the hot steam of the bear's breath on my neck. The testimony of David's victory jarred me out of the tunnel-visioned terror I was in. I had enough of listening to fear. I stopped running and slowly turned around to face the massive beast... and certain death. I had no sling or weapon of any kind. All I knew was that Holy Spirit said to face the beast and that I could beat it. I looked into the cold piercing eyes of the bear, and then... I blinked. When I opened my eyes, the great beast was dead! I became more aware of the strong presence of Holy Spirit. He told me that all He needed was a willing vessel. If I would just agree with Him... He would do the rest! He was only waiting for me to give Him my "yes". I didn't need to strive or do anything in my own power. All I had to do was step out. I didn't have to DO anything... there was no striving or fighting. And then I woke up from my dream.

As I woke up, the revelation was washing over me... I didn't have to do anything other than obey Holy Spirit and face the bear (symbolic of my fears). My attempts to escape the bear got me nowhere, but once I obeyed Holy Spirit... all I did was blink! It didn't matter that fear manifested physically. Jesus was still KING. I couldn't see that fear had no power and no authority over me... until I obeyed Holy Spirit and faced the bear! Fear has nothing on Jesus, so fear has nothing on me. THAT was powerful.

LIVING FROM PERFECT LOVE

Fear destroys our joy and peace. It puts us into fight or flight mode, which clouds our thoughts with unsound perspectives. Obviously, the opposite happens as we begin to be free from fear. The fruit of the Spirit becomes more present and tangible in our lives and often feels like there is a bubble of God's goodness surrounding us. We CAN live from Perfect Love in every area of our life. It IS possible to live totally free from fear. As we choose to agree with Jesus instead of fear, fear will begin to sound more and more unsound. Living from Perfect Love is a long journey, but it is very rewarding!

Recently I prayed against a tornado (yes, in the physical, not a vision) that was forming above my house, and it stopped within seconds. That normally would have been a "scary" situation to be in, but fear never crossed my mind. I had a dream the night before about stopping a tornado, and the next day Yahweh told me that one was forming right outside my house. I wasn't afraid, and I already knew what to do because of the dream I just had. I went outside and commanded the tornado to stop. I shouted into the sky, "There will be no destruction in Jesus' name!" My children even came out to join the tornado-stopping party. We all saw the funnel coming down...and then we watched it miraculously suck back up into the sky right after we commanded that there would be no destruction. It wasn't scary at all... it was FUN!

Being a son of God IS fun. We don't have to live reactionarily to the world and all the bad things that happen. We are powerful and can make powerful choices. As we grow out of fear and into love, life becomes more fun. Life isn't just about having fun, but God did intend for us to live in joy and bliss. When Yahweh created the garden, He could have named it anything, but He named it "Pleasure"! (*Eden means pleasure.*) Yahweh's desire, still to this day, is for us to live in bliss and pleasure, crushing it as sons of God.

Jesus lived in and from this Perfect Love that we have been discussing. Before His death, Jesus faced many "scary" situations, and yet nothing shook Him. Jesus was anchored in perfect love. Even in the face of pain and death, there was a joy that He carried...

> Hebrews 12:2 (TPT) "We look away from the natural realm and we focus our attention and expectation onto Jesus who birthed faith within us and who leads us forward into faith's perfection. His example is this: Because his heart was focused on the joy of knowing that you would be his, he endured the agony of the cross and conquered its humiliation, and now sits exalted at the right hand of the throne of God!"

> Hebrews 13:6 (TPT) "So we can say with great confidence: 'I know the Lord is for me and I will never be afraid of what people may do to me!'"

It IS possible for us to live free from fear! We don't have to take on fear in "scary" situations. There are no "scary" situations from Heaven's perspective... and Heaven is where we LIVE from! We don't have to take on trauma. Stopping the tornado was fun, but there will be things we face that won't be "fun". What Jesus faced at the cross was not fun in any regard, but He had joy and unshakable peace. There was nothing to fear even in the midst of what He said. Jesus is our example in everything. I am confident that we can go through ANYTHING without partnering with fear or trauma.

Now when I look back at all the traumatic events that I have experienced, ALL I see is Jesus. All I see is His face, and all I feel is His joy. EVERY pain and memory that we bring to Him can be healed and redeemed so much that we can look at the event and feel NO pain or trauma. It is POWERFUL to see our worst memories healed and redeemed. And the same healing and breakthrough I have experienced are available to you (and MORE!). I am not special. Jesus died so that NONE would perish. The only thing "special" about me is that I chose, and still choose, to receive Yahweh's love and truth that He pours out to all of us. You can do the same thing. You can choose to lay aside the offense and accusation against God and pursue Him beyond the pain. If you are willing to lay everything aside and go after Jesus, I can confidently say that it will change your life. I chose to pursue a personal relationship with Yahweh because I realized that He was the only healer. What I found was far more precious than just healing for my soul... I found Yahweh Himself.

Psalm 23 (TPT)

1. Yahweh is my best friend and my shepherd. I will always have more than enough.

We live from abundance through our relationship with Yahweh.

2. He offers me a resting place in his luxurious love. His tracks take me to an oasis of peace near the quiet brook of bliss. That's where he restores and revives my life. He opens before the right path and leads me along in his footsteps of righteousness so that I can bring honor to his name.

His OFFER is rest, peace, and bliss. It's an offer that requires us to agree with Truth. He doesn't force it on us! When we accept His offer, He restores and revives our life.

3. Even when your path takes me through the valley of deepest darkness, fear will never conquer me for you already have! Your authority is my strength and my peace. The comfort of your love takes away my fear. I'll never be lonely, for you are near.

We decide who conquers us: fear or Yahweh.
His love takes all our fear, and we are never alone

4. You become my delicious feast even when my enemies dare to fight. You anoint me with the fragrance of your Holy Spirit; you give me all I can drink of you until my cup overflows.

   He is our FEAST in the midst of our enemies. The presence of our enemies doesn't take away from what the Lord has given us. Notice all the things He does for us in this verse.

5. So why would I fear the future? Only goodness and tender love pursue me all the days of my life.

   All fear is gone, and all that is left is His pursuit of us all the days of our life.

Perfect Love Casts Out Fear

Self-Application

KEYS TO REMEMBER

- Fear is our enemy, and choosing to agree with fear brings death in our life.

- Fear can be boiled down to 1 of 5 roots: Fear of death, fear of pain, fear of lack, fear of rejection, and fear of failure. And each of these core roots has a different truth from Yahweh to counter the lie.

- Perfect Love casts out fear because Yahweh's truth (which is Perfect Love) is the only thing powerful enough to counter the lies of fear.

- Just because the fear *feels* true and can be validated by our experiences does not mean it is TRUTH. Yahweh determines what is and isn't truth, not our circumstances or feelings.

QUESTIONS TO ASK JESUS

- How do I get free from fear?

- In what areas of my life do I not trust You?

- What fears in my life would You like to talk about today?

- Which of the 5 core fears am I ready to receive truth on?

(This one is important to do ONE at a time. Jesus will have different answers for each root fear which is why it is important that they be addressed individually. It takes TIME for our soul to receive the truth. You can use the steps referenced earlier in this chapter, or you can ask Jesus how to deal with each fear you bring Him.)

- What do You want to tell me about fear?

- What does fear look like in the spiritual realm?

Remember each of these questions can be used as a springboard to identify lies, break agreement with them, and receive Jesus' truth instead. Please also reference Chapters 5 & 6 of The Foundation for help and troubleshooting blocks when trying to talk to Jesus about fear.

Chapter Three

REJECTED
OR ACCEPTED?

I was in junior high when my world imploded. I exposed some perversion going on within my only friend group. To my shock, as things came to light, the adults/parents turned on me. All but one of my peers/friends rejected me, which snowballed into every social outing bringing an attack from one or more people. I eventually just stopped going to anything other than church events. A few years later, I was then rejected by that church because my beliefs outgrew their box. I carried the pain and effects of their rejection with me... until I went to the winter camp I mentioned earlier. After my first encounter with Yahweh, I began to be more and more hungry for freedom. The more life I experienced in my soul, the more I wanted to be healed of all my soul wounds. I brought Jesus my pain, fear, and memories of rejection... and His answer/healing shocked me.

Rejection is a tender topic for most people. At one point or another, almost all of us have experienced rejection. Rejection seems especially common around the teenage years. As painful as it is, the rejection in and of itself is not the issue... HOW our soul processes rejection determines if it is painful or not.

For example, let's say you see some toddlers playing a game, but they won't let you join in. You would probably laugh at the circumstance and brush it off. After all, they are just toddlers. But what if your good friend rejected you? That type of rejection would probably cut very deep. In both circumstances, you faced rejection, but you received it differently.

Rejection itself doesn't cause the soul wound. What we DO

about being rejected determines if it becomes a soul wound or not. Our soul filters EVERYTHING that happens through its worldview. If our soul, knowingly or unknowingly, looks to people for validation and affirmation, then how people treat us will greatly affect us. What we don't realize is that when we don't receive the affirmation and validation that Jesus gives us, we will look to get it from people. Our soul then interprets how people treat us as identity statements.

When I was trying to wrap my mind around the reality of rejection, Jesus showed me a picture of His life. Again and again, HE was rejected. Jesus was PERFECT love in the flesh! No sin or darkness in Him, and yet He was despised and hated by people. In all that Jesus faced, the betrayal... rejection... and hate, He never took it personally. He didn't receive an identity statement from those broken people because He knew the truth. Only what the Father says truly matters. Why would Jesus believe an identity statement from someone who is lost, blind, and hurting? The answer is easy and clear for Him. I too am made in the Father's image, and I can walk in the same perspective that Jesus had. He knows my innermost being better than I do. All things are known and seen by Him. He is GOOD, and thankfully HE gets the final say. There is no arguing with what Yahweh declares. He is the author and finisher. Yahweh says I am loved. I am HIS... accepted... beloved... cherished... and fought for! THIS is the truth.

Hurting people hurt people. They are bound and blinded by soul wounds. When someone acts out from their pain, it furthers the cycle. We can choose to enter that cycle and dysfunction, OR we can bring the hurt to Jesus to see what HE says about it.

To be clear, we are both accepted AND rejected. We are accepted, loved, cherished, and fought for by Yahweh. And we are/will be rejected, hated, and despised by some people, just like Jesus was. What happens to us doesn't define us. Even our own actions and choices don't define us. Yahweh defines us, and His definition lasts forever. It comes down to one thing... who are you going to believe? Will you receive an identity statement from broken people, or will you receive your identity from Yahweh Himself?

> John 15:18 (TPT) "Just remember, when the unbelieving world hates you, they first hated me."

BREAKING OFF THE IDENTITY STATEMENT

All this *sounds* good, but how do we walk it out? When we hear a lie long enough, it *feels* like truth. This is the challenging part of any soul wound we face. When we have years, sometimes decades, of rejection's identity statements that we have agreed with, then TRUTH sounds like a lie. When Jesus told me that rejection wasn't my identity, it *felt* false. I WAS rejected by people. My soul had a long list of facts and experiences that validated the identity statements of rejection. Here's the issue, while facts are true... they are not TRUTH. **Spiritual truth supersedes physical facts.** Even though I was rejected, rejection was not who I truly was. I am adopted by the Father... fully accepted and fully loved. THAT is the truth. The things that happen to me and the things I choose to do are concrete facts, BUT they do not define who I truly am. What Jesus was saying WAS true, and He was calling me out of the lies I believed.

It was a FACT that Lazarus died. It was a FACT that he couldn't come back to life. TRUTH said a different word, and TRUTH superseded FACT. There was concrete evidence; it was a done deal according to the worldview. Heaven's view was and is different from the worldview. Spiritual truth always trumps natural law because it is a higher reality.

We live in a dual reality: a spiritual and physical realm. WE decide which reality we will agree with and live from. To break off the old identity statements of rejection, it requires us to choose to disregard the FACTS and cling to the TRUTH instead. Breaking off the old identity statements of rejection requires us to receive what Jesus says instead of what the world or circumstances say. Rejection may be a fact in your circumstances, BUT we are defined by CHRIST, not what happens to us.

The process of breaking off the rejection identity statements is a very similar process to how we dealt with fear...

- Bring the identity statement or lie to Jesus and ask Him about it. You can ask things like:

    o   Who do YOU say I am?

    o   What do You think about this identity statement?

    o   How does Your truth supersede facts?

- Then the choice is yours to keep agreeing with the lie that is causing death in your heart, or choose to believe what Jesus said regardless of how true it *feels*. In encounters, sometimes the lies are portrayed as objects like chains or tar. The lies can also personify into a being. Jesus understands what we need to receive and understand His truth. So, He is careful and intentional with how He reveals every lie and soul wound to us. Either way, I like to face the lie and say something like:

    o   I have decided that YOU are my enemy. Your goal is to bring death and destruction to my life. I choose to no longer agree with the lies you have been telling me. Your facts don't determine my value.

    o   I repent (which Biblically means to change the way you think about something) and choose to receive and agree with what Jesus says instead.

- And just like I mentioned with fear... usually, the first two steps will need to be repeated multiple times. The soul doesn't easily forget what it has been clinging to and how it has been operating for years. It doesn't matter how many times we have to take the lies to Jesus. Each and every time is a victory and a step forward towards our soul believing truth.

Please also reference Chapters 5 & 6 of The Foundation for help and troubleshooting blocks when trying to talk to Jesus about rejection. These steps are the basic process for dealing with lies our soul believes. There are other ways to do this, but in my experience, this has been the easiest way. Then as we grow and mature, Jesus will show us new and shortcut ways to heal our souls.

LIVING LOVED

I had a very intense but wonderful encounter with seeing Jesus when He was flogged. Throughout my life, I have seen plays, movies, and artwork of the crucifixion. They all portrayed a common picture: Jesus being heartbroken by the betrayal and downcast by what He faced. The moment right before His death was portrayed as the ultimate betrayal when he cried, "My God, my God, why have you forsaken me?". Religion says that God "abandoned" His only Son because He "couldn't look upon sin". This teaching/explanation didn't sit well with me, and I was very thankful for a fresh perspective on the crucifixion. What I saw in the encounter was a COMPLETELY different scene...

In the encounter, Jesus reminded me that it was with JOY set before Him that He faced the cross (Hebrews 12:2). I saw Jesus POWERFULLY making every call. HE told Judas when to go to the religious leaders. HE stayed silent before Pilate. (*If He had spoken, TRUTH would have been revealed, and Pilate would not have ordered Him crucified!*) Jesus was NOT disheartened or discouraged. First, there is no discouragement in Heaven, so we will not find it in Jesus! Secondly, in the most radical love story in all the universe, Jesus saw the joy of His reward... His bride... before Him and endured the cross in confident peace. I saw Jesus being flogged, and He was... RADIANT. Jesus was beaming... glowing with radical love, joy, and confidence. Jesus received every whip and knew that He would use it for OUR healing. Jesus' eyes of fire pierced the soul of every soldier who attempted to flog Him. His love was fighting for them, forgiving them before the whip even broke His skin. The soldiers could only get one or two flogs in before being overwhelmed by love to the point of having to stop flogging. Then I saw another soldier would step up to take their place... only to have the same fate. It took many, many soldiers to get the lashes completed. Jesus was not powerless in the flogging. It was one of the most powerful things I have seen. I was wrecked and overwhelmed, but the encounter went on...

Jesus was CONFIDENT in what was about to take place. So much so that He told the thief on the cross beside Him that they would be together in paradise that day. Jesus then called out to the Father and asked for forgiveness for the people because they did not know what they were doing. Then the sky went dark, and I saw the sins of the world laid on Jesus. In that moment, I understood that Jesus was yielded ONLY to the Father. He ONLY did what He saw His Father do, which means Jesus never yielded to sin. That is why the Father had to LAY the sins on Jesus. Jesus took on our sins, felt them, and bore them. Even though He was ONE with the Father, Jesus, bearing our sins, turned HIS face from the Father. The moment Jesus took on our sin, HE chooses to hide just like Adam did. Because of this, Jesus experienced the same separation that we cause because of our sin. That is why He called, "My God, my God, why have you forsaken me?" Notice Jesus didn't call Him "Father" while He was bearing our sins — He called Him "God". Jesus fully took on and fully understands our blinded and broken hearts... and then He conquered sin! How do we know? In Jesus' last words, He had CONFIDENCE in Yahweh once again and called Him "Father"! He broke through the sinful nature and was confident in His relationship with Yahweh as He declared, "It is finished. FATHER, into Your hands I commit my spirit." And with that, the encounter ended.

It was so clear to me that God never abandoned His Son. Jesus said multiple times that He and the Father were ONE. There can be no separation in ONENESS. What I was told by religion was wrong. Jesus wasn't rejected... and neither are we.

> Psalm 27:10 (NLT) "Even if my father and mother abandon me, the Lord will hold me close."

Rejected or Accepted?

Self-Application

KEYS TO REMEMBER

- We will be rejected by the brokenness of people in this life, but we don't have to receive rejection as an identity statement.

- TRUTH supersedes FACTS because the spiritual realm is a higher reality than the physical realm.

- We decide whose identity statements we are going to agree with. It's our choice... wholeness or brokenness.

QUESTIONS TO ASK JESUS

- What do you say about rejection?

- How do I not receive the lies of rejection when someone rejects me?

- What do you say about the areas of my body and heart that I reject about myself?

- How do I break free from the wrong identity statements that I have been believing?

Remember each of these questions can be used as a springboard to identify lies, break agreement with them, and receive Jesus' truth instead. Please also reference Chapters 5 & 6 of The Foundation for help and troubleshooting blocks when trying to talk to Jesus about fear.

Chapter Four

I WILL NEVER LEAVE YOU

Loneliness. It's one of those deeply painful soul wounds that eat at our soul. I don't think it's a far stretch to say that every single person has felt lonely at some level. When we are hurt, our human reaction is to build a wall around our pain. The walls we build are intended to keep the pain from infecting the rest of our hearts and prevent further pain. The problem is that walls _feel_ like they keep everyone (*and healing*) out while the pain festers and spreads within our hearts. This then develops into deeper and deeper feelings of... loneliness. Since this world is filled with hurting people who are hurting others, I can safely state that everyone has felt loneliness to varying degrees.

In my life, I *felt* very alone even though I was surrounded by friends and family. The walls I built in my soul were compounded by my unusual supernatural experiences. I felt misunderstood and alone in the midst of a sea of people. Being with people was nice because it distracted my soul from the constant pain and torment. But somehow, I still felt alone with people and even more when people weren't around. I had heard verses my whole life about God never leaving us or forsaking us, but no matter how much I read these verses, I couldn't shake the feeling of being alone. As I learned how to engage with Jesus, a hunger grew for inner healing. In spite of the encounters I was having with Jesus, my feelings of loneliness kept coming up. My loneliness *felt* tangible... I couldn't tell if it was a crushing weight or an ominous void in my soul, but it was painful nonetheless.

When I began my journey of becoming whole, there was a

phrase that Jesus said often to me: "If it's not found in Heaven, then it doesn't have to be found in you." I took to heart what Jesus said and used that statement to filter the emotions and feelings in my soul. I would ask myself, *"Is there fear in Heaven? Is there shame in Heaven? Is there loneliness in Heaven?"* As I took every thought and emotion captive, I evaluated them from that perspective. I decided that if Jesus didn't choose those emotions, thoughts, and feelings, then neither would I!

When loneliness came up, it was obvious that it was a lie, but how would I shake the *feeling*? I knew the *feeling* was a lie, but it felt real. Every time I felt alone, I chose to go to Jesus and allow Him to heal that dark, painful part of my heart. Not only did I have to bring Him the pain, but I had to make the choice to AGREE with the truth Jesus was giving me at that moment: I WAS unknown and misunderstood by my friends and family, but not by Jesus. I FELT alone and in lack, but the truth was that I was ONE with YAHWEH Himself. I am in the Father, and He is in me. I am one spirit with Jesus, and I am filled with Holy Spirit. That doesn't even include the host of angels and a cloud of witnesses all around. It IS a party everywhere I go. THIS is my reality.

None of what Jesus told me *felt* true at the beginning. My walls were blinding me to the truth and reality that was ALREADY within me. Walls are an interesting soul reaction because the *intention* for putting walls up is to self-protect from more pain... but walls actually compound the pain and blind our souls to healing! We then become MORE hurt because we *feel* rejected by God... even though we were the ones to put the walls up and attempted to push God away in the first place.

Cool note: it is IMPOSSIBLE for there to be any separation between us and God. We CAN'T push God away... He is in everything and holding all things together. So, when we put the walls up, Jesus sits WITH us in the dark and pain of our soul while we sit there feeling rejected by Him and alone. Our walls blind us to the reality we ALREADY have with Jesus, and they bind us to the festering pain we feel.

ADDRESSING WALLS

In my head knowledge, I *knew* that I wasn't alone... but I *felt* the complete opposite. To deal with the loneliness, I had to deal with my walls. I felt so isolated, unknown, and alone within my walls. I was yet again at a crossroads... Would I take my walls down and "let" Jesus in? OR would I stay self-protective and keep the walls... and my pain? I had already decided that I wanted Jesus more than anything. He had my "yes", so I chose to take down the walls. I was terrified, and to be honest, I didn't know if Jesus would be big enough. I didn't know anyone else personally that was actually free from their soul pain. At the time, I didn't even know that I had access to abundant and eternal life on this side of the veil!

My walls were towering, thick, and made of stone. They didn't let the light in. I could see Jesus knocking on the walls of my heart, but I felt naked and exposed to the idea of taking the walls down. I felt powerless and lost as to how to even begin such a big project. I had spent years reinforcing these walls; how long would it take to bring them all down? Nevertheless, my heart was set on Jesus, so I pushed past my fears and decided to ask Jesus where to begin.

First Jesus explained that it was important to break agreement with all my walls and their "duties" of protecting me. I acknowledged that the walls were hindering my healing and breakthrough. Even though I thought they were protecting me from pain, I admitted that they were actually keeping the healing out, leaving me stuck in pain. I said something along the lines of, "Soul, we acknowledge and decide that this wall is not helpful. It is a trap for us. So right now, I choose to no longer partner with this wall."

After that, I felt led to ask Jesus how to take down the wall. Jesus may take it down Himself (with our permission), or sometimes He will tell you how to do it. In my case, Jesus gave me a tool to take down my wall. Once my attachment and desire to keep the wall were removed, I was able to take it down with the object

Jesus gave me. (I am intentionally not revealing the object so you don't have a preconceived idea of what type of object Jesus might give you to take down your own walls.) I have been told that it is helpful to make sure the entire wall is gone, not just partially. Because of this, I was thorough in my taking down all of the walls to the point that I couldn't see any bricks left. The light that I was blinded to now flooded my heart. I could feel the warmth of Jesus on my skin. He felt so close, so kind, and so loving. The terror I felt in taking down the wall was gone. Jesus yet again proved that choosing Him is always worth the cost.

Even though I had already dealt with some fears and soul wounds at that point in my journey, this was yet another layer deeper of healing and freedom. My fears were relieved, and I didn't feel naked or exposed in the light. In fact, I felt covered, covered by Love Himself. I could see that Jesus was indeed big enough to remove all the pain and torment I bore. Now that the walls were gone, I could bring my feelings of loneliness to Him.

Once I chose to take down my walls, I felt truly known and seen for the first time in my life. I could feel Perfect Love all around me, permeating my very being. That day wasn't the last time I felt lonely, BUT it was the beginning of my freedom from the lies and torment I was in. There was still a process I went through to renew my mind and learn a new way of thinking/living. My soul still had a habit of meditating or thinking about lies instead of truth, but I was hooked on feeling so good and so alive in Jesus. Taking my walls down was a marked moment in my becoming whole. With each layer and breakthrough, I was tasting more of the goodness of God, and each time I became more hungry for abundant life!

Taking our thoughts captive and renewing our minds is a new way of living. We are called to daily pick up our cross. Each time we feel anything that is not of Heaven, we can bring it to Jesus and see what He says about it. Over time, the feelings of loneliness and being unknown will be replaced with a wholeness that is beyond words.

SATISFIED

It feels strange to say I am satisfied, but that is the best English word I can find to describe what I feel now. I no longer feel alone, isolated, or unknown. There is no longer a deep and gaping void in my soul that feels like it will never be healed. I am complete, fully known, and fully seen by the Father, Son, and Holy Spirit. It IS a blissful party everywhere I go.

Loneliness is not a physical condition, but rather a soul perspective that brings death to our life if we agree with it. Our circumstances don't determine our feelings of loneliness. Our soul beliefs and perspective determine our feelings... regardless of circumstance. For example, many people think that once you get married and have a family you will feel fulfilled. While marriage or kids may be the fulfillment of a dream, those things cannot fix the root lies of loneliness. You can feel just as, or even more alone within marriage than without a spouse. In fact, I don't know of a marriage where one or both spouses don't feel isolated, unknown, and alone. Our deepest desire is to be fully seen and fully loved... and a spouse will always fall short of that. If you are looking for marriage or a friendship to fix your loneliness, then you will probably begin to feel even more alone because the original loneliness is now compounded by your disappointment. We were created for oneness and intimacy with Yahweh. All other forms of intimacy will fall short because nothing comes close to the fullness and satisfaction we find in Jesus.

It is literally IMPOSSIBLE for us to be alone. Heavenly realities supersede physical circumstances. Even if someone was totally isolated from people on an island, there is so much community, family, and connection found in Heaven that a person can live in radical abundance regardless of their circumstances. We are in, and one with, Yahweh, Jesus, and Holy Spirit. Every need is provided for, the table has been prepared, and our cup is overflowing. Anyone can choose to feel lonely while seated in Heavenly places... but that is far from reality. The more we realize and agree with our oneness in Jesus, the fuller and more satisfied we will grow to be. Jesus IS big enough for everything we face. We CAN live in and from abundant life the moment we choose to!

I Will Never Leave You

Self-Application

KEYS TO REMEMBER

- We feel alone behind the walls we build around our pain. Our walls push people and even our perception of God away while trapping us in with the festering pain.

- In spite of strong feelings of loneliness and isolation, our true reality is oneness with Jesus.

- As we renew our minds and take down our walls, we will find ourselves more whole and satisfied than we ever thought possible! YAY, God!

QUESTIONS TO ASK JESUS

- Do I have any walls that I have built?

- What is the cost that I am paying by having those walls up?

- (If you are ready to take the walls down) Will You help me or give me a tool to take down my walls?

- What do You say about my feelings of isolation and loneliness?

  o Break agreement with the lies and choose to receive what Jesus says if you are ready to be free from loneliness.

  o Repeatedly bring Jesus the feelings of isolation and loneliness until you stop feeling them altogether.

- Is there anything else You want to tell my heart or show me about this?

Remember each of these questions can be used as a springboard to identify lies, break agreement with them, and receive Jesus' truth instead. Please also reference Chapters 5 & 6 of The Foundation for help and troubleshooting blocks when trying to talk to Jesus about fear.

Chapter Five

THE GIFT OF
FORGIVENESS

I had an encounter addressing unforgiveness that put the Fear of the Lord in my heart. I was deeply hurt by a friend whom I was very close with. She had sinned against me... repeatedly, and the pain and offense grew in my heart towards her. My friend was dying and was only acting out because of the fear and pain she was in, but the more she acted out, the more hurt I became. Instead of focusing my eyes on Jesus, I became fixated on the offenses and unforgiveness. This all led to a very intense and emotional encounter. Before I share the experience, I do want to mention that this particular encounter required a very unique circumstance to make it even possible...

I was pacing in my room (which was something I often did in this season) while I was mulling over my painful circumstances. Suddenly I looked up and, in the spirit, I saw a well-dressed man in my room. His hair was trimmed, and he looked sharp. He smiled and held his hand out to me... waiting for me to give him something. At first, I didn't realize that he was a demon. He wasn't repulsive and obviously evil like demons usually appear to me. When he reached his hand out to me, I saw that I was holding a rolled-up paper in my hand. I instantly knew that I was holding the death certificate of the person whom I was so hurt. (In visions, there is sometimes an understanding that your soul has even though no explanation has been given.) The well-dressed demon was waiting for me to simply lift my hand to give him the death certificate. I knew that I didn't even have to say anything in the spirit. Simply the intention of my heart, the slight lifting of my hand in the spirit, was all that was needed...

and then my pain would be over. That person actually would have been taken out of my life. The relief of my pain coming to an end filled my mind. I could have my life back, but I also knew the weight of her death would be on my shoulders. I had been so fixated on my pain that I couldn't see the Father in this vision. I could feel Him standing right behind me. I still couldn't see Him, but I could feel the Father's warmth and love. In spite of the pain, I knew I didn't want to partner with the demonic or with death. Even though it meant the pain would be prolonged in my circumstances, I wanted to partner with Yahweh instead of death. I carefully and intentionally lifted the death certificate up over my head behind me to hand it to Yahweh. I still couldn't see the Father, but I felt Him take the death certificate. The demon turned and walked away. And the encounter was over.

After the vision ended, the reality of what had just happened hit me like a ton of bricks. Her life hung in the balance, and I was close enough to her to be a factor in her life or death. It was such an intense experience, and I wondered if it was just a vision or if it would have physically happened. The next day she called to tell me that she had almost died at the same time I had the vision... it WAS a cross-dimensional encounter! I thought the encounter was intense before... but now it was all the more real and made me sick to my stomach. The demon was looking for someone to partner with death towards that person because all she needed was a little push... and she would have given in to death. I was SO close to giving the demon her death certificate. It was so tempting, and yet, in spite of my pain, I chose to partner with life instead of death

I want to mention again, that this was a very unique situation. Most of the time, our choice to hold onto unforgiveness does NOT amount to us being a factor in someone's life or death. I think it was because I was so close to her AND because she was already so close to death that it made it possible for me to affect her life and death.

Unforgiveness actually binds us TO the person we are holding unforgiveness towards. We carry responsibility as sons of God, and we can aid or hinder (never prevent though) someone's healing and breakthrough. Our forgiveness (or lack of) affects their healing and freedom by making it easier or more resistant in the atmosphere around them, tipping their scales towards choosing life or death. So, in my circumstance, because she was so close to death AND because we were so close, I had enough influence to make the difference between her life and death. On a much less drastic scale, it is still true that our forgiveness or unforgiveness aids or hinders other people's healing journey.

The encounter I had put the Fear of God in me about the unforgiveness I was carrying in my heart. I never realized that unforgiveness affects more than just us. It binds us to the wrongs against us, affects the atmosphere around us, and can even affect the person who sinned against us. It can be very painful to address our unforgiveness, but it is also incredibly healing... and the healing extends beyond our own souls.

LET THERE BE JUSTICE!

To fully dive into learning about forgiveness, I would like to first discuss our justice heart. Our desire for justice is a common root of our unforgiveness and is the same reason why we reject the idea of forgiveness. We were created to have a sense of justice. It is something we were all born with. We want things to be fair, and we want the wrongs to be made right. Even within the world of criminals, often they have their own (skewed) code of justice. Even though criminals may break the law regularly, there is usually a self-created code that they live by. If someone wrongs them, they will retaliate out of that core need for justice. Everyone wants justice to be served, and that is why forgiving someone can be SO hard.

When we are wronged, we want there to be justice. We were hurt or taken from, and now we want justice to be done on our behalf. Our natural reaction is to deeply desire the "scales" to be balanced or made right. We want an eye for an eye and a tooth for a tooth. Abel was slain unjustly, and his blood cried out from the ground for justice. Anytime our blood is spilled, our natural reaction is to cry out for justice. But for sons of God, our old reaction/nature has been redeemed for a HIGHER nature. Jesus' blood speaks a better word. His blood cries out for mercy, and HIS blood is now in our veins. As sons of God, we are also born again into a HIGHER justice system. Justice in Heaven looks very different than the demand for blood we see on earth.

> Ephesians 2:6 (NLT) "For he raised us from the dead along with Christ and seated us with him in the heavenly realms because we are united with Christ Jesus."

As sons of God, we are seated in heavenly places. We once fell short of the glory of God, but through Christ, we are made like Him. We can live from the heavenly system we are seated in OR live from a myriad of worldly systems. A system is a set of rules and government within an area or group. There are many systems which you can decide to live from. Countries have systems, families have systems, and cultures have systems. Every worldly system falls short of the Kingdom of Heaven. It's important to understand that sons of God are called to operate from a higher system than the worlds. Heaven's system brings reconciliation through mercy and the blood of Jesus, whereas the world's system demands punishment through judgment and the need for blood.

If you ask or demand judgment against a brother, then you are choosing to operate within a lower, worldly system. What most people don't understand is that YOU are also subjected to the same system you want others to be judged in. YOU decide which system you live in and from: mercy or demanding justice. You can't live in mercy for your wrongdoings and ask for justice for someone else at the same time...

> Mark 11:25 (ESV) "And whenever you stand praying, forgive, if you have anything against anyone, so that your Father also who is in heaven may forgive you your trespasses."

Matthew 6:14-15 (ESV) "For if you forgive others their trespasses, your heavenly Father will also forgive you, but if you do not forgive others their trespasses, neither will your Father forgive your trespasses."

We can receive forgiveness and give forgiveness, or we can refuse to forgive and bind our souls in brokenness. The choice is ours, and it is a weighty one. Will we demand blood for blood in an earthly system model? Or will we agree with Heaven's model and receive the blood of Christ that settles ALL debts and demands?

To be clear, justice is not bad. Yahweh IS just, and there is justice in Heaven. There WILL be judgment, and everything WILL be made right. Yahweh is FAITHFUL and He is GOOD in all He does. We can trust Yahweh and have confidence that all the evil in the world will be addressed. He is not turning a blind eye, and He will get the final say. Yahweh is the Alpha and Omega, the beginning and end.

Deuteronomy 32:4 (BSB) "He is the Rock, His work is perfect; all His ways are just. A God of faithfulness without injustice, righteous and upright is He."

Psalm 9:7-8 (BSB) "But the LORD abides forever; He has established His throne for judgment. He judges the world with justice; He governs the people with equity."

Our sense of justice becomes misplaced when we take justice into our own hands. Man-made justice systems are corrupt, blind, and filtered through the perception of our experiences. When we take an eye for an eye, we are left with a bunch of blinds and hurting people. Man's justice focuses on balancing the scales, but Yahweh's justice focused on reconciliation and restoration. This is Heaven's system that we are born into...

Ephesians 1:7 (ESV) "In him we have redemption through his blood, the forgiveness of our trespasses, according to the riches of his grace"

Isaiah 43:25 (ESV) "I, I am he who blots out your transgressions for my own sake, and I will not remember your sins."

2 Corinthians 5:19 (NLT) "For God was in Christ, reconciling the world to himself, no longer counting people's sins against them. And he gave us this wonderful message of reconciliation."

Believe it or not, God wants justice even more than you do. He does not make light of the unjust and wrong things done against you. He is a GOOD Father, and He takes GOOD care of His kids... all of them. To begin to understand the Father's heart on justice, we first must be willing to surrender our idea and demand for justice. Only then will our hearts be open to hearing and growing in Yahweh's heart and perspective.

When we hold onto the unjust areas of our lives, WE are submitting our hearts to be in continual torment by those unjust things. It wouldn't make sense if someone stabbed you and then you chose to keep the knife in your body until justice was served. Instead, you would take the knife out, get medical help, and let your body heal. This is the obvious and logical thing to do, but we hold onto the knives in our hearts without thinking twice about it. We often wait for justice to be served, for the wrongs to be made right, and only then will we allow the knife to be pulled out so our hearts can heal. We keep our heart stunted and wounded when we intentionally (and even unintentionally) don't address the areas where our heart feels stabbed.

There are unjust things that happen continually on the earth and those things could easily consume and overwhelm us. There is much evil and brokenness around us, but God made a way for us to not be overwhelmed or consumed by them. The way is called forgiveness. Only then can we begin to see the Father's desire for reconciliation, the beauty of Heaven's justice system, and the purity of justice that is coming to the earth.

THE GIFT OF FORGIVENESS

*To forgive: to let go of all the negative emotions
we carry regarding a person, group, or event.*

Forgiveness is a GIFT because, without it, we would be crushed from carrying the pain we experience in this world. Forgiveness is the way out of the pain. It is freedom from the weight of the unjust things we have faced. The past will no longer control your life, demand your energy, and steal your peace.

One of the reasons the Bible tells us to forgive is because unforgiveness affects OUR hearts, OUR health, and OUR peace. When we choose to forgive, we are freeing our hearts and allowing that painful area to be healed. We choose to pull the knife out and allow Jesus to heal that area of our hearts. Until we choose to forgive, we are choosing to be subject to our past. Our past becomes our present because we bring our unhealed past into our current situations.

Forgiveness is letting go of all the negative emotions that affect our hearts. When we choose to forgive, it does NOT condone the offense that happened. It is not sweeping it under the rug and pretending it didn't exist. Until we give it to Jesus, we carry the weight and pain of the event. The weight of the injustice is tiring to our souls and quickly turns to resentment, bitterness, anger, rage, and other negative emotions in our hearts. These emotions fester in our souls, and begin to harm our bodies as well. Forgiveness is choosing life and freedom, and it is choosing to trust God's justice system.

> *Romans 12:19 (NLT) "Dear friends, never take revenge. Leave that to the righteous anger of God. For the Scriptures say, "I will take revenge; I will pay them back," says the LORD."*

> *Proverbs 10:12 (ESV) "Hatred stirs up strife, but love covers all offenses."*

1 Peter 4:8 (ESV) "Above all, keep loving one another earnestly, since love covers a multitude of sins."

We have been forgiven much. Our old nature died along with all our sins. We now have the blood of Jesus in our veins, and we can agree with the higher system we live in. Because of Christ, we have the supernatural strength and ability to forgive and be like God. We can live free from pain and untied to the past. We can live in and from mercy instead of living in and from pain.

Forgiveness is our new identity in Christ. It is who we TRULY are, and as we embrace it, we will become more alive and whole than we thought possible. Forgiveness becomes the new perspective from which we live and view life. It empowers us to see beyond someone's actions and instead see the pain and brokenness of THEIR heart. It separates the person from their actions and grows our capacity to see them as Yahweh does. Yahweh does not define us by our actions, and forgiveness empowers us to do the same. Regardless of how we *feel* about it, forgiveness is healing, freeing, empowering, life-changing, and a vital step towards a breakthrough for our ever-growing hearts. As difficult as it may be, it actually is MORE difficult to stay bound and deceived by the pain.

HOW TO FORGIVE

Like all emotional healing, forgiveness is tricky to address because it is an invisible concept. How do you know if you actually let it go or if you are still holding onto it? In the physical world, you can SEE what you are carrying. When it comes to the spiritual world and our emotions, it comes down to feeling and intention. This is why self-awareness is vital for soul transformation. Regularly checking to see how our emotions, feelings, and thoughts are doing is part of becoming a healthy son of God. Anytime you feel angst, bitterness, frustration, fear, or anger towards someone, shows an area of your heart that is carrying hurt.

Forgiveness is not easy, but it is possible. To forgive goes against our soul's desire to get even and requires us to trust that Yahweh knows best. Nevertheless, we received forgiveness, so it is possible for us to extend forgiveness. It is a choice and a process, but if we trust Jesus and choose to extend forgiveness, we will find healing and breakthrough in our lives and journey.

To begin the journey of forgiving, there are 3 groups to individually evaluate:

- Forgiving Others

    o This is the most obvious group to cover when talking about forgiveness. Any person or group that you feel bitterness, disgust, anger, or fear towards, shows an unhealed part of your heart holding onto the past. It may have been from childhood or just last week. The soul remembers and holds onto painful things until you choose to let them go and allow Jesus to heal the pain.

- Forgiving Yourself

    o Forgiving yourself can be more difficult than forgiving others. You have to live with yourself and your choices. While it is important for us to take responsibility for our actions, it is MORE important for us to extend to ourselves the same grace and forgiveness that Christ gives us. Unforgiveness only brings death to our souls. There is no life or good thing that comes from self-punishment and refusing to let go of the past. Jesus forgave us and doesn't remember our sins. So, do you think you know better than Christ? Are your ways better than His? If not, then it's time to forgive yourself and free yourself from the past that Jesus has already forgotten. It can be so hard to receive the love and forgiveness for ourselves, but it is finished! And now we are invited to be free from the torment we are holding over ourselves.

- Forgiving God
  - Starting off, I want to be clear that I am not claiming that God has sinned against us or done anything wrong. He is perfect and everything He does is GOOD. That being said, we can still be hurt and carry offense even though He hasn't done anything wrong. The perceived hurt from God is a real hurt to your soul. You may feel like God didn't "show up", be mad that He "didn't answer your prayer" how you wanted, or hold Him responsible for something bad that happened. Whatever is causing the offense and anger towards God, that area will cause a block in your relationship with Him and will keep you from being healed. God doesn't need you to forgive Him, but your heart needs to let go in order to be whole. You can be honest with how you feel. You can be real with Jesus in your anger, disappointment, or whatever else you feel. He already knows it's there, so it's silly to avoid the elephant in the room. Be honest, choose to surrender the pain and offense towards God, and let the healing begin.

Once we have recognized an area of our heart that is holding onto pain, we are at a crossroads. We can decide to forgive, let go of the past, and let the healing process start. OR we can choose to leave the knife in a little longer and prolong the pain. The choice is up to us. When we are ready to let go and forgive, it is helpful to know a few things:

- **Forgiveness is a CHOICE more than a feeling**. In this aspect, it is very similar to love. Commonly people talk about love as a feeling, but to truly love someone, we choose them in spite of our feelings. In 1 Cor. 13, we are told that love is patient, kind, does not envy or boast, is not self-seeking or easily angered, and doesn't keep a record of wrongs or delight in evil. This definition of love is an ACTION. It is an intentional choice. Yes, there may be feelings involved, but the feelings do not define love. In the same way, forgiveness is a choice, usually long before it is a feeling. The first time we forgive someone, we don't usually feel better immediately. We choose to forgive out of obedience and to free our hearts from death. The feelings of forgiveness will come in time, but they do not define our forgiveness. Likewise, they are not an indicator of whether we truly forgave or not. I can truly love my husband while not having fluffy lovey feelings. Does it mean I don't love him when I don't feel fluffy feelings? NO. I choose to love him. The choice to love defines love, just like the choice to forgive defines forgiveness.

- **Forgiveness is a process.** Usually, the bigger the pain, the longer it takes for your heart to fully let go and not pick up the pain again. Your heart's autopilot is to carry the pain you are working on releasing. After you forgive the first time, your heart will most likely pick the pain back up simply out of habit. This often leads people to think that "*it didn't work*" when they forgave the first time. EVERY time you forgive and let go, you are allowing healing to flow in your heart. Forgiving someone "works" every time because it is a moment when you choose Jesus instead of holding onto the pain. This being said, don't get discouraged. Forgiveness takes time to retrain what our heart holds onto… the pain or Jesus. For big pains, you may need to choose to forgive over and over. Every time you forgive there is a breakthrough and healing, but because of the depth of the pain, your heart may need to let it go multiple times before it eventually chooses to not pick up the pain again.

Note: While it is normal for forgiveness to take time, it is possible for our soul to let go of all the pain at once and never pick it up again! "Lump sum" forgiveness becomes easier as history is built with Jesus. As our soul's capacity to trust Jesus grows, ALL inner healing becomes quicker and easier! Yay, God!

- **Forgiveness is a form of surrender**. Any pain that we choose to hold on to, keeps that area of our heart from healing because we have not surrendered the knife.

- **Forgiveness is IN your blood**. You have a new nature, and Jesus' blood speaks a better word. You have the empowerment and ability to forgive as a son of God. If you feel like you "can't", you can ask Jesus for help and for perspective. He has given you everything you need for healing, even the strength to forgive. You CAN forgive. It may be hard, and you may have to do it over and over, but Jesus' blood is in your veins. You can do this.

- **Forgiveness is a command.** (Colossians 3:13, Ephesians 4:32, and so on) Everything Yahweh asks of us is for GOOD and not for evil. Similar to the command "Do not fear", the command to forgive is vital for the health of our soul. It is easy to justify unforgiveness because of our justice heart, but in spite of injustice, death is still released in OUR heart by choosing unforgiveness. This is why it is a command.

Steps Of Forgiveness:

- Acknowledge the reality that unforgiveness brings death to our souls. Personally, this helps remind my soul that even though there was an injustice, I don't want to partner with death in my life.

- Choose to obey the command to forgive. To forgive, I go on an encounter and give the unforgiveness, and the event over to Jesus. I choose to let it go, and because I am such a visual person, it is helpful for me to see the handoff in an encounter. *Note: There are usually many people that we need to forgive and usually multiple things we have to forgive ourselves and God for. These steps will need to be applied to each area of unforgiveness until your soul is willing to give it all in one lump sum. I also* find it very helpful to ask Jesus how HE views the person and what happened. It's always very enlightening to see things from Heaven's perspective, and it helps my soul more quickly release the unforgiveness as I see Jesus's heart for that person.

- REPEAT until there is no more angst in your soul. The greater the injustice, the more times we will need to forgive before our soul decides to fully let it go. Our soul subconsciously may pick up the hurts again, and this is why we usually have to repeatedly forgive and bring things to Jesus.

When we bring our desire for justice to Jesus, He grows our capacity to trust Yahweh and HIS justice. Justice is not wrong, but man's idea of justice brings death while Heaven's idea of justice brings life. In spite of all Jesus faced, His cry was for mercy. As we surrender our demand for blood, we begin to see through the eyes of mercy. Stuffing or dismissing our justice heart stunts our healing.

> Luke 23:34 (TPT) "Father, forgive them, for they don't know what they're doing."

The more we forgive others, the more we begin to see the world from Heaven's perspective. Evidence of our forgiveness will begin to manifest as our heart heals. Some proof of forgiveness would be that you can think about the person/event without your stomach churning or your heart aching anymore. Incredibly, forgiveness is not just a neutral feeling towards the person, but a shifting of the heart to the point of seeing the person as the Father does. You will also have more peace and confidence in Yahweh. Every time we encounter Jesus, we gain a little more insight and understand a little more about how the system of Heaven works. It takes time to undo all of the frameworks and broken lenses we grew up with. Little by little our justice heart will be healed and will look more and more like Jesus.

In addition to healing our justice hearts, living from forgiveness is the only way to stay healthy in the midst of a broken world. The invitation for the sons of God is to live in full agreement with Yahweh and His truth. No circumstance is big enough to pull us out of our agreement with Heaven. It is OUR choice moment to moment what to partner with: life or death. This world is filled with hurting people who are hurting people. The more we see through the eyes of love, and agree with Heaven, the more we become unshakeable.

The Gift of Forgiveness

Self-Application

KEYS TO REMEMBER

- Yahweh GAVE us our justice heart. Our desire for justice is not wrong, but it is misplaced when we demand blood.

- There are 3 different groups to look at when addressing unforgiveness in our soul: unforgiveness towards God, people, and ourselves.

- Unforgiveness brings death to US, which is why forgiveness is a command so we can live WHOLE and free from death.

QUESTIONS TO ASK JESUS

- What does forgiveness look like in the spirit?

- What does unforgiveness look like?

- What does it look like for me to surrender my justice heart to you?

- How do I forgive?

- Is there anything that I am angry at You about?

  o *I suggest starting with forgiving God. Unforgiveness towards God affects our ability to encounter God, AND it hardens our hearts against Him. I suggest going through the steps listed in this chapter and start with forgiving God first for any offenses you feel towards Him. After forgiving God, then it will be easier to encounter God in regard to forgiving others and yourself. Please also reference Chapters 5 & 6 of The Foundation for help and troubleshooting.*

- Is there anyone in my life that I am holding unforgiveness towards?

- Are there any areas in my life that I need to forgive myself for?

Remember each of these questions can be used as a springboard to identify lies, break agreement with them, and receive Jesus' truth instead. Please also reference Chapters 5 & 6 of The Foundation for help and troubleshooting blocks when trying to talk to Jesus about fear.

Chapter Six

THE WAY OUT
OF SADNESS

Before I dive into my story of how I learned the way out of sadness, I want to mention that this chapter was hard for me to write. The struggle was NOT because I talk about my miscarriage, but because the pain has been so far removed from me. I don't feel the pain from that season to the point that I didn't even remember the despair I felt. Jesus has healed my heart, and now all I see is Jesus when I look back at the miscarriage. All I see is His face and His love piercing the core of my being. To write this chapter, I had to ask Yahweh to remind me of the pain and torment that I was in. It was a very intense and painful season, but Jesus was big enough to heal my soul and body to the point that I didn't even see or remember the pain.

During my miscarriage, Yahweh taught me how to not get stuck in pain. The way out of the sadness is through grieving, also known as mourning. I didn't value grieving or even understand what grieving was prior to losing my son. I went through a miscarriage while being a radical lover of Jesus. Don't be misled into thinking that hard times will not come because you are a believer or are extra "spiritual". Hard times and persecution are guaranteed in this life no matter who you are.

> John 16:33 (NLT) "I have told you these things so that you may have peace. <u>In this world you will have trouble,</u> but take heart! I have overcome the world." [Emphasis mine]

The more we accept the truth in this verse, the sooner we can be anchored in peace, even in hard times. And if we do become overwhelmed by an event, then our healing is quicker because we have a history with Jesus and tools already established in our hearts. I was shaken to my core during my miscarriage, but I was met by Jesus in such a powerful way. I was amazed to see that Jesus was big enough to make me whole after being so broken.

We were so excited to be having another baby. Everything was wonderful... until the bleeding started. I prayed and prayed and prayed against it. I released Heaven, rebuked demons, bound curses, went to the courts of Heaven, and used every spiritual strategy I could think of. I had friends and family members praying. The bleeding finally stopped, but I still didn't know if I got a miracle or if the worst had happened. It was especially painful because it took the doctors a full 30 days before they confirmed that I had indeed lost the baby. For 30 days, I waited in agonizing limbo — not knowing if my baby had survived or not. Finally, to my despair, I got my answer. My son was gone.

The pain of losing my son was like nothing I had experienced before. The despair, the crushing sadness, the confusion I felt towards God. I knew that God didn't cause my son's death because of some judgment against me. In attempts to comfort me, people said things like "Jesus takes the best ones", but I knew that wasn't true. I knew Jesus was big enough to heal me and save my son. So why didn't He? Why didn't He stop it? Why weren't my rebukes and bindings enough to stop Satan? Why didn't God give me the strategy and Heavenly wisdom to stop the miscarriage? As a friend of Jesus, I was tormented by these questions and crushed by my pain. My heart hurt beyond what words could ever articulate. All I could feel was pain and loss. I didn't FEEL like talking to Jesus. I was exhausted after 30 days of fighting for my baby — only to be devasted that it wasn't enough to save my son. Furthermore, I was conflicted about accepting the miscarriage. God is the God of impossible things. He could put my baby back in my tummy, right? Could I save my son even after the miscarriage if I prayed a little more or had a little more faith? I felt lost in a sea of pain and tormenting questions.

In my devastation, I had a choice. Would I get angry and pull away from God? Or would I turn to Him in spite of my pain and the accusing questions that ran through my head? I knew that Jesus was the only Healer. I knew that He truly was the only way out of my pain. If I didn't want to get stuck and harden my heart, I had to turn to Jesus. I also knew that I needed Him more than I needed answers. Answers don't bring healing to a broken soul; they only answer the cry of our mind to understand. But understanding is not enough. The pain would still be there in my soul even if I had answers. I knew Jesus had to be big enough to heal me EVEN in the face of losing my son. I didn't want to be stuck in my great pain. So, I chose Him.

For the first time in my life, I grieved with Jesus. I cried until I couldn't cry anymore. I felt like an empty shell, lost within myself. But still, I chose Him. I chose to engage with Jesus, even though my heart was too sad to hold a conversation with Him. I would go on an encounter and lay everything down on my altar in Heaven. My pain, my questions, my confusion, my anger... everything was laid down. Then, I chose to walk away from the altar and go sit with Jesus. We sat in silence together most of the time. My heart hurt too much to talk. So, I sat with Jesus next to a brook, choosing to not pull away from Him. The natural response is to pull away when we are in pain. I had to be extra intentional in that season to not shut down and pull away because of the pain I felt.

Matthew 5:4 (BSB) "Blessed are those who mourn, for they will be comforted."

Every time I felt the pain of the miscarriage, I brought it to Jesus and engaged with Him. Again and again, I laid it down and went, and sat with Jesus. In the beginning, I was continually and constantly bringing my pain to Jesus. Over time, it began to lessen. Every minute turned to every hour. Every hour faded to a few times a day. Slowly, the pain was healing. After 30 days of intentionally grieving with Jesus, I felt whole again, and that's the only way I can describe it. It will never be ok that my son died. Death is the enemy of God, and it was an evil thing that happened. But I was no longer ruled by the pain of losing him. I was at peace in spite of what happened. Jesus made me whole.

I Choose You

In spite of my feelings
In spite of my questions
Still, I choose you

In times of abundance
In times of devastation
Still, I choose you

Even when pain blames you
Even when I can't see
Still, I choose you

In sickness and in health
For richer or for poorer
I will still choose you

Where else could I go?
Only you have the words of life
There is no one like you

Where else could I go?
Only you are the healer
The only redeemer

So, I lay it all down
I give you my all
Let it be a burnt offering
Pain and all

I choose you
Again and again, I will choose you

I choose you
Because you first chose me

TO GRIEVE OR NOT TO GRIEVE?

To grieve: to face the sadness and accept the painful reality of where things are currently — so that there can be healing through Jesus.

Pain is inevitable in this broken world, and pain is something we run from in western culture. We HATE pain, and usually process pain in two dysfunctional ways... either we stuff it, or we wallow in the pain until it becomes our identity. Neither of these processes are ways to grieve. Most people equate sadness with grief, but grieving is actually the way to heal sadness! If we don't grieve, then we will be stuck in sadness. Grieving is the way to not be overcome by a broken world. We have the ability physically and emotionally to let the pain out so our soul doesn't break from its weight. Grieving is a powerful GIFT from Jesus because it is our way out of pain.

Sadness and pain can be caused by an array of things from the loss of a loved one, to disappointment over a circumstance, to a trauma happening to us, or even hearing about trauma happening to a stranger. The list of things that can cause us pain is infinite. And if we didn't have a way to get the sadness out, then we would be crushed by it over time. We would become more and more dysfunctional if we were left unhealed. This is why grieving is a gift. There is a way out of the pain.

We cannot grieve if we ignore the pain. This is a common way to handle sadness in western culture. Grieving, also known as mourning, is letting your heart be present in the pain so you can process it and heal. But most people try to grieve without connecting to Jesus or they rely on time to heal it. "Time heals all wounds" right? No, it doesn't. In fact, it can't. Jesus is the only Healer. Any other attempt at healing is a facade of comfort for our wounds. "Time heals all wounds" may feel like it's healing, but it is only allowing a callous to grow over the pain. That's why you don't "feel" the pain as much... because it's callousing. Time doesn't make us whole. The wound is still there even if it is numb. That is why when something triggers the pain, you fall apart all over again. There wasn't a true healing... your callous just got ripped off.

The key is to grieve WITH Jesus. He is the only Healer, the only way to be made whole again. And you CAN be made whole, without pain, because Jesus is that big. Heartache is unavoidable, even for Jesus. He makes Himself vulnerable to us by choosing to love us. He knowingly exposes Himself to pain and heartache for our sake. He knows better than any of us what wholeness in the midst of heartache looks like. He sees ALL of the horrible things happening on the earth at once. And He loves all of us more than we can possibly imagine. He knows heartache on an immense scale. He is also big enough to heal each and every pain we have and will ever face.

Grieving with Jesus is a process, and it takes TIME. So be patient with your heart while it heals. In Jewish culture, it is expected that you grieve for 30 days. You are not shamed for crying or wailing in public. In Israel for example, if you break down crying in a store and there is no one to mourn with you, a stranger will come and mourn with you — to be with you in your grief! How beautiful and precious is that? The 30 days is not a formula, but it is the cultural standard of the Jews. In my personal experience, 30 days is about what it was for me to feel whole again. It's not an exact number, it can take longer or shorter to grieve something. Everyone's grieving journey looks different, but either way, it will take time.

There are many things to grieve, but some of them may be surprising to you.

Grieving the loss of a loved one

- This is definitely the most commonly understood form of grief. When we lose a loved one, the heart-crushing sadness, confusion, anger, and depression are what most people think of when they think of grieving.

Grieving a traumatic event

- There is a devastation that settles into our souls when we experience trauma. Trauma can come from abuse, losing a house, physical injury, loss of body parts, or losing a job. There are an infinite number of circumstances that can happen to traumatize our souls. The pain of these events gets trapped in our souls, and stunts us if we don't bring it to Jesus. Choosing to grieve events is just as important as grieving the loss of a loved one.

Grieving an unfulfilled hope — a disappointment

- This is probably the most foreign and ambiguous thing to grieve. Outside of losing a loved one or experiencing a traumatic event, your heart may need to grieve something that it has invested emotional energy into. For example, if someone spends years hoping that their spouse would change and it doesn't happen, they become disheartened. Another example would be the disappointment from breaking up with someone that you had dreams of marrying. Any hope or dream that we have emotional energy invested into, can become a disappointment and therefore stunt our healing.

  Proverbs 13:12 (BSB) "Hope deferred makes the heart sick"

  To be clear, HOPE is not wrong. But WHERE we put our hope either sets us up for health or disappointment. When we put our hope in people and circumstances, our emotions are subject to those circumstances and how they turn out. If what we hoped for doesn't happen, then our hearts will become sick and stuck. As believers, our hope is intended to be in Jesus. People and circumstances are unreliable in this broken world. Even when everything around us is falling apart, Jesus isn't shaken by the storm. He is our Anchor, our Rock, and our Help. If we place our hope in something other than Jesus and it doesn't happen, that deferred hope is the thing to grieve so we aren't stuck in sadness.

Hope deferred is an intangible but very real thing to grieve. It is also very painful to let go of things we have hoped for. Many times, we have years of emotional energy invested into them. The same level of emotional energy you invested into a desire, is the same level of grieving needed for your heart to heal and come to terms with that disappointment. It feels wrong at first like you are "giving up hope", but that is not what you are doing. You had misplaced hope that made your heart sick, and now you are placing your hope on the only steady and constant thing in all the universe — JESUS!

Culturally, grieving is not valued or understood, so there is all the more pressure to just stuff the pain and "move on". Grieving is painful and uncomfortable. And naturally, we run from painful things. If we don't let the pain out of our souls though, it sours and stunts our hearts from growing. Sadly, pain is unavoidable in this world. BUT Jesus gave us a way out of the pain! Jesus gave us grieving as a precious gift so we could be made whole, even in a painful world. From little pains to big pains; whether grieving a loss, an event, or a deferred hope — Jesus wants to heal ALL of it. He wants all of our hearts to be whole. The weight of carrying around sadness and pain is exhausting; this is why Jesus wants us to bring everything to Him — big and small things.

> John 14:27 (BSB) "Peace I leave with you; My peace I give to you. I do not give to you as the world gives. Do not let your hearts be troubled; do not be afraid."

To say you will "always be sad" or you will "never be ok", means you have a very small view of Jesus. People say these sorts of things to express the pain that's in their souls, or to try to give honor to the lost loved one. But their honor is misplaced, and it becomes a word curse that traps them in a cage of sadness.

To agree with "I will always be sad" or "I will never be ok after this" binds your soul to torment... while at the same time saying that Yahweh is just not big enough. That lie becomes your self-created reality if you agree with those statements. Though the statements may feel real, they are tormentors waiting to bind you. Take your thoughts captive and submit everything under Truth. Jesus IS big enough for you to be whole. It will take time... but it is available to you.

One last thing, God is NOT in control! Or at least... He is not in control in the way religion teaches it. People often fall back on the phrase "God is in control", but He isn't. Yahweh is all-powerful, all-knowing, and has all authority, BUT He chooses to give us "control". He is not some puppet master behind the scenes causing everything to happen. Yahweh did not kill my baby nor did He cause all of the evil things that happen in this world. Jesus came so that sickness and death would be eradicated from the earth. To blame God for everything evil in the world is to accuse the only Healer and Source of life in all the universe.

> James 1:17 (BSB) "Every good act of giving and every perfect gift is from above, coming down from the Father of lights, with whom there is no variation or shadow of shifting."

Blaming God only hardens our hearts against Him. As long as we have free will, there is always the ability for evil to happen in the world. So, in this way, God is not in control. We are. Broken people partner with hell and bring evil into the world every single day. So, let's not blame our Healer and Savior for something He didn't do, and instead let's run to Him! Jesus has all authority and does have the final say. Amazingly, Yahweh promises to work all things out for good, and He always keeps His promises.

Grieving is messy and painful. Our soul scrambles for answers to the confusion while trying to find a solution for the pain it feels. It's hard to function when all you see is pain. But as you bring your pain to Jesus, He is faithful and big enough for every... single... thing you bring Him. You can be whole and free from the pain.

HOW TO GRIEVE

To grieve: to face the sadness and accept the painful reality of where things are currently — so that there can be healing through Jesus.

Learning how to grieve is not hard... CHOOSING to grieve and making it a priority is hard. Sitting or wallowing in pain is not grieving. Grieving does not mean just crying. Crying lets the pain sit on the surface for the moment, but it does not bring healing. And "moving on" is not a sign that you are done grieving and your soul has healed. Crying, stuffing, numbing, callousing, wallowing, distracting, or any other coping mechanism is only a way of managing the pain. When used long-term, coping quickly grows into surviving. There is only one way to truly heal. His name is Jesus. There is no healing outside of Jesus. There is no life outside of Him.

There is one vital key for healing — you grieve WITH Jesus. Jesus may teach you a different grieving tool and may take you on a totally different healing path. If you get one thing out of this book, I hope that it is understanding how vital it is to grieve with Jesus, our Healer. He is the Way, the Truth, and the Life.

Below are the steps I used to grieve. Please keep in mind that this is not a formula. These are the steps Jesus took me through to heal, but He may take you through different steps or in a different order...

1. <u>ACCEPT</u> where things are at. If you refuse to look at the pain and face your current reality, you won't be able to heal. You can't heal something that isn't there. So, you first have to admit that the pain is there so that you can grieve it. Denial and deflection are not your friends. They are coping mechanisms that keep you in pain. Accepting and facing the pain is vital and necessary in your healing journey.

2. BRING EVERYTHING TO JESUS. Not just the pain —
   bring Him your questions, your anger, your confusion,
   your disappointments... all the messy emotions, and yes,
   even the accusations you feel against Him. Be honest,
   raw, and transparent with Jesus — He already knows the
   mess is there so let's get it out on the table so it can be
   healed!

   The pain will be at its worst in the beginning, so you will
   be constantly bringing your pain to Jesus. It may even
   be minute by minute. Then as you heal, you will feel the
   pain hour by hour. The key is that EVERY time you feel
   the pain, you bring it to Jesus. As time goes on, your
   heart will heal and you will slowly feel the pain less and
   less. It will fade to a few times a day, then once a day,
   and keep dwindling down until you don't feel the pain
   anymore.

   Personally, I bring everything to Jesus in an encounter
   (covered in The Foundation, Book 1). It helps me to
   be able to see my pain tangibly in an encounter. I lay
   everything on the altar and then walk away from the pain
   and questions to go be with Jesus. You don't have to do
   this in an encounter. At first, it may be too painful for
   your soul to see. You can audibly tell Jesus all the things
   you are bringing to Him. You can write them down or
   find a way that works well for you. The important thing
   is that you are intentional to engage your free will and
   bring everything to Jesus.

   Note: Remember that if you are harboring offense against
   God, then your heart is hardened towards hearing from
   Him in an encounter. Bringing the enemy's lies and
   accusations against Jesus is different from agreeing
   WITH the accusations and lies. When we lay things
   down with a softened heart, we are ready to receive and
   hear what Jesus has to say. But when we are mad, hurt,
   and pointing the finger at God, that is when our heart is
   hardened from receiving from Him.

3. <u>CHOOSE JESUS OVER DEMANDING ANSWERS.</u> Bill Johnson puts it beautifully: "To have peace that surpasses understanding, you must first give up your right to understand." As much as we <u>want</u> the questions answered, the answers won't and can't bring us peace or healing. Especially in high-pain circumstances, the "need" for answers become an idol and bondage to our hurting soul. The answers themselves aren't wrong to have, and they will come in time. But they become a stumbling block to us, and THAT is what I am highlighting to you. Choosing Jesus instead of demanding answers, FREES us to be healed and whole in ways we never knew were possible. Jesus is truly all we need.

4. <u>STAY WITH JESUS</u> until you feel your heart soften and shift. This part can be time-consuming when we are in deep pain, but this is the quickest way through the pain. It is POWERFUL when we fix our gaze on Jesus until our heart shifts. The shifting of the heart is hard to explain because it is intangible. I would describe the shift as a melting of the pain and a surrender to Jesus. Usually, the pain doesn't completely go away the first time, but the heart does soften. It's like an anchoring peace quietly begins to carry the weight of the pain so your soul can breathe.

The crucial part of grieving is surrendering it all to Jesus. The goal is to bring everything to Him so that everything can be healed. In a beautiful exchange, Jesus gives us joy for our mourning; beauty for our ashes; and wholeness for our pain. His goodness knows no limits. As believers, we are invited to be fully surrendered to Jesus — not holding anything back. It's important to know that anything we hold back from Jesus brings death into our life. It changes everything when we choose to shift our eyes off of our pain and onto Jesus. The pain lessens at that moment and the healing begins. Personally, my goal was to stay in the Presence until all I felt was Jesus. That was powerful for me, and I think the catalyst for why I was able to heal in just 30 days.

Because we don't value or understand grieving in western culture, we want to get back to our lives and move on. Trudging through pain, bringing it to Jesus, and waiting there long enough until our heart shifts, feels like a lot. Grieving well takes time, and it requires us to be intentional. Being patient with yourself is one of the hardest but most important things about grieving. Pain will keep popping up as you heal, and it is easy to focus on the wound instead of bringing it to Jesus. The more intentional you are to grieve, the faster you will heal. Your healing journey is up to you. Every grief you stuff and ignore remains in your heart. The quickest way out is to intentionally bring every pain to Jesus and STAY there until it shifts. It is very time-consuming at first, but this is the fastest this way out of the grief. If you stuff pain, it is hard to access it later. You may not live in a culture that values or understands grieving, but you can choose to value and prioritize grieving in your own life even if no one else does. The steps are simple. If you grieve well, then you will heal. You will have peace again and feel whole.

Note: In the grieving process, it will be helpful to strategize with Jesus to see how best to grieve in your life circumstance. Each of our lives is unique, and Jesus has a perfect strategy for our healing. All we need to do is ask Him!

HELPFUL KEYS FOR GRIEVING

- RETRAINING HABITS. In the process of grieving, it is important to retrain your soul's habits. If the soul's habit was to run from pain, then it is important to be intentional to retrain your soul's reaction to heartache. Often times our soul runs on autopilot, pre-programmed with how to handle things that come up: run from pain, use coping mechanisms, pretend everything is ok at church and on social media, and "fake it 'til you make it" (the problem is we never make it). We do these kinds of things repeatedly, only to find ourselves coming around the same mountain again and again, wondering why we are stuck. Running from pain only prolongs the pain.

The quickest way out of sadness is to go through the waves of pain with Jesus. To change our habits, we must be diligent to watch our emotions and bring them to Jesus as they come. The goal is to train the soul to run to Jesus for everything. Then ultimately, the intention is to learn to LIVE in Jesus and abide in Him. So be intentional and present, bringing everything to Jesus as it comes. Over time, this will retrain your soul's habits and you will begin to run to Jesus instead of running away from the pain.

- ACCESSING OLD PAIN. Most of us have old pain that we didn't process in the moment. Our soul has been trained to run from pain, stuff it in a box, and bury it — hoping it never comes up again. The problem is these buried things don't go away and they poison the soil of our hearts. Buried heartache will sour and fester into more pain and dysfunction, which starts affecting more and more areas of our soul. Getting these areas healed can be tricky, but nothing is too big for Jesus.

  Accessing old pain can be difficult because the soul has been trained to ignore it. Basically, you are trying to force your soul to revisit areas that it has intentionally avoided. Sometimes there is the grace to do it, and you can successfully dig up old stuff and bring it to Jesus for healing. This is wonderful when it happens. But more often than not, our soul is very efficient at locking away the pain, and it remains a locked vault when we try to access it. In this case, there are a few ways that I have discovered to heal buried pain:

  1. The simplest way to heal buried pain is to wait until the pain surfaces. Buried pain never goes away. It is always there, festering deep in our hearts. One day or another, that pain will get triggered by an event or memory. When it comes up to the surface, then you have the tools and practice to deal with it! Just like everything else,

bring it to Jesus and go through the grieving steps. Waiting for the pain to trigger and resurface requires time and patience, BUT again and again, I see the Lord's kindness in it. Healing takes time. Though waiting to be triggered might not seem ideal, Jesus and His timing are perfect. In the meantime, you will be building history and trust with Jesus in other areas. He knows what our soul can and can't handle, and Jesus doesn't rush us. So, waiting for the pain to surface is actually ok and works out, because either way, we are doing it with Jesus.

2. Sometimes Jesus will dig up the pain Himself. Jesus knows how to access that pain and everything that is needed to heal it. He is more than able and willing to do it! BUT our soul is not always willing. Jesus will not go against our soul's desire and free will. Even if part of your soul wants healing, a larger part of your soul may want that pain to stay buried. Remember that our soul is divided into real estate with voting power. Our soul often blocks healing because some parts of our soul are not ready to trust Jesus and let go of the brokenness. All this to say, sometimes it works to ask Jesus to dig it up, and sometimes it doesn't.

    Important note: When inner healing feels like "it's not working", this shows that our soul is so shut down that it is not ready to address this area. God is not withholding from you. Jesus IS big enough and quite literally died so you can be made whole. And the enemy is not powerful enough to keep you from being healed (more on that is coming in the next book). The enemy would LOVE for you to "give up" because "it's not working", but that is a LIE designed to keep you broken for as long as you will stay there.

Our healing journey happens at the pace of our soul's willingness (free will) to open up and trust Jesus. The more history we build, the more the soul is willing to trust Jesus with more painful areas. Remember that we are becoming whole, renewing our minds, and growing up in Christ. It won't happen in an instant. The process is beautiful and precious to Jesus. We are growing priceless history in our relationship with Jesus, Yahweh, and Holy Spirit. It's not about getting to some spiritual destination or about some self-created idea of healing that you want to achieve. We joined in a marriage with Christ. And in a marriage, you get to love one another and live together forever. It's not about what you do and how fast you do it. It's about who you are, and who you are with.

3. Lastly, you can ask Jesus to heal the pain (in a lump sum) without you having to see it or feel it again. This is wonderful when it happens, but you miss out on your soul-building history with Yahweh. To be out of pain without any work is everyone's preference. It's fast, easy, and clean. But we don't learn and grow when this happens. There are times that Jesus will come and heal buried pain all at once, but more often than not, Jesus will walk through our pain with us because of the priceless fruit it grows in our souls.

The way out of sadness takes time and patience. It is worth the work, and what you gain with Jesus is priceless. Keep your eyes fixed on Jesus, and everything will be ok. Happy grieving.

POST GRIEVING

Revelation 21:3-5 (BSB) "And I heard a loud voice from the throne saying: 'Behold, the dwelling place of God is with man, and He will dwell with

*them. They will be His people, and God Himself
will be with them as their God. He will wipe away
every tear from their eyes, and there will be no
more death or mourning or crying or pain, for the
former things have passed away.' And the One
seated on the throne said, 'Behold, I make all
things new.'"*

We have great hope as believers. Everything will be made new.
One day there will be no more death, no more pain. Though it
may not feel like it, the Bible says this life is a vapor. What feels
like a long time on earth, is just a blink compared to eternity.
This hope is an anchor, and this hope is something to fix our
eyes on so that we don't get dismayed by all the pain in this
world.

There was a season in my life when I lost three friends in a short
amount of time. Each of them died slowly and painfully from
cancer, and they all passed away two weeks apart from each
other. I had spent years fighting for them, praying for them, and
contending for their healing. It was a slap in my face and a slap
to my faith to have the three of them die slowly and so close
together. My heart was broken, to say the least. I followed the
steps of grieving and while in an encounter, I asked Jesus to
give me a new understanding of death. I needed truth to stand
on in the midst of such painful loss after we prayed for a miracle
but didn't see it happen. Below is the account of what Jesus
showed me. Small details were changed to protect the hearts of
those involved, but the heart of the vision remains pure.

*Jesus first stood in front of me to give me an
illustration of death. Jesus was facing one
direction and said "This is your time on earth. You
are conscious of this world and your focus is here."
Then Jesus turned and faced the other direction.
"Death is simply turning around. The point of
existence stays the same, you are just as alive
as you were before. The difference now is that
your consciousness and focus are in the spiritual*

realm instead of the physical realm." Then Jesus turned to face me so He could see both directions at once to reveal a deeper mystery. "Some people learn to live in both worlds at once. They can be fully conscious in both realms. And some people learn to take their physical body back and forth as well!" Enoch and Elijah came to mind when Jesus said that. Then Jesus added, "Don't worry though, for those who don't learn to live in both worlds and their body dies, they will go back and get their body later."

My mind was spinning, and I was so encouraged to see a new perspective on death. It was not a loss, but merely a changing of their consciousness from this world to Heaven. Yes, we will miss them, but it is only for a time, then everything will be made new, even their body! But the encounter wasn't done yet. In the vision, Jesus brought me one of my friends who had just died. I was SHOCKED to see her. She was so young, healthy, whole in the soul, and GLOWING! She looked GREAT! I shouted out, "Kerry! Oh my goodness! It is so good to see you! I am SO sorry I couldn't heal you or raise you from the dead. I tried my best." Kerry was glowing and smiling the biggest smile I have ever seen. She said to me, "Jessica, it is FINE! It was nothing."

"NOTHING", she said? I saw her die. I saw Kerry slowly and painfully wither away from surgery after surgery and treatment after treatment. I saw Kerry's spouse slowly die of cancer earlier. I didn't understand, so I asked, "NOTHING? How can you say that was nothing? That was a terribly painful and horrible way to die." Kerry, unfazed and still glowing answered, "Jessica, all I see is Jesus when I look back at my time on earth. I don't see or feel the pain. From Heaven's perspective,

I can truly say it was nothing." I had a small grid for what Kerry was talking about. My memories of sexual abuse have been re-written by Jesus. When I look back at my memories now, all I see is Jesus, and all I feel is His peace. There is no more pain or trauma. Jesus has healed those moments in my life. So, when Kerry told me that all she sees is Jesus, I had a grid for understanding what she was talking about. If Jesus could do it for my traumatic memories, of course, He could do it for Kerry's whole life. Then I remembered Kerry's kids. Now they have lost BOTH parents to cancer in a short amount of time. So, I asked Kerry about her kids. Her answer blew me away even more...

Kerry smiled even bigger than before (which just made her glow more) and said, "Jessica, my kids are going to be just fine! There is no fear in this realm. Jesus is so big and so good. My kids are in GOOD hands. Everything will work out for good." When Kerry said that I instantly knew that that didn't mean her kids wouldn't face hardships. Kerry had unshakable confidence and peace in Yahweh. Jesus was good to Kerry's kids and loved them even more than Kerry did. So even in a broken world, her kids were in good hands. And if they didn't get healed on that side, they were going to experience the same healing and breakthrough that both their parents did on the other side. Everything would be fine and made new.

After the encounter ended, I quickly realized why Jesus had to bring Kerry to me. With my level of faith at that time, I would not have believed Jesus if He had told me that Kerry's horrible suffering was nothing. I had to hear it from Kerry herself — that her time on earth was nothing, and all she can see now is Jesus. Jesus was so kind to meet me at my faith level so that I could receive a life-changing encounter.

This encounter was a marked moment in my life. I saw another facet of the goodness of God. Once again, Jesus blew me away with His wonderfulness. Everything really was going to be ok, even in this painful and broken world. Healing is available to us, and if we don't figure it out, Jesus is big enough to redeem it all. Either way, everything will be just fine. Whether we walk as mature sons and keep our bodies as we explore the realms, or we love Jesus but die a slow and painful death — either way, Jesus is good. He will get the final say, and Jesus will fix all this one day. There will be a pain in this world for now. But it will not last.

I was also excited to discover the potential of living in the same peace that I saw in Kerry. I saw that it was possible for me to live from Heaven to earth with unshakable confidence and peace EVEN in the face of tragedy. I was given the invitation to live from a Heavenly consciousness and perspective. Over time, I realized how powerful this perspective is and the difference it makes in my prayer life. My prayers aren't a reaction to tragedy anymore. Instead, I am one with the Father, abiding in the Father, and I ask Him in confidence what He wants me to do. I still don't see 100% of what I pray for come to pass, but all I see is Jesus. I see the bigness and goodness of God woven into everything, and I am confident that Jesus can and will fix everything one day.

Jesus has overcome the world. He has gone before us and has given us everything we need for healing and wholeness. He is big enough for everything we face. He gave us grieving as a gift so that we have a way out of the pain. We also have confidence and hope because Yahweh is VERY good and He isn't done yet.

> *Isaiah 61:2-3 (TPT) "I am sent to announce a new season of Yahweh's grace and a time of God's recompense on his enemies, to comfort all who are in sorrow, to strengthen those who are crushed by despair and who mourn in Zion — to give them a beautiful bouquet in the place of ashes, the oil of bliss instead of tears, and the mantle of joyous praise instead of the spirit of heaviness..."*

The best is yet to come beloved! There is always hope!

The Way Out of Sadness

Self-Application

KEYS TO REMEMBER

- Pain is unavoidable in this life, but grieving is our way out of the sadness and pain.

- There are 3 different areas in our hearts that can be stuck in sadness: the loss of a loved one, traumatic events, disappointments/unfulfilled hopes.

- Demanding answers from God is a stumbling block to our soul. When we choose Jesus over answers, we free our hearts to heal and be free from grief.

- To be whole, we grieve with Jesus and bring Him every pain until it doesn't hurt anymore.

- The more quickly and thoroughly we bring Jesus our pain, the faster we will heal and be made whole.

QUESTIONS TO ASK JESUS

- Are You big enough to heal my grief?

- Do I have pain/sadness over losing someone or something that I loved?

    o How do I grieve this pain?

- Do I have pain or sadness over any traumatic events in my life?

    o How do I grieve this pain?

- Do I have any pain or sadness over any unfulfilled hopes? Anything that I am deeply disappointed about?

    o How do I grieve this pain?

Be intentional to bring each pain to Jesus and stay with Him until you feel your heart shift. Reference the "How to Grieve" section if you are feeling stuck in the grieving process. You can also reference Chapters 5 & 6 in The Foundation for help with encountering Jesus.

Chapter Seven

INSECURE TO SECURE

Due to many events in my early childhood, I was a very insecure child and teenager. Similar to how I hid my fears, I never showed my insecurities. I refused to look weak. I looked people in the eyes, held my head high, and gave a warm, but firm, handshake when I met people. I acted confident, but it was all a mask. Deep inside I wanted to please people, was insecure about my identity, and I hated many parts of my body.

Insecurities take root anytime we feel vulnerable, weak, ashamed, or uncertain in our hearts. If we feel insecure about something, it shows us an area where we are not aware of, or confident in, Yahweh's thoughts in that area of our life. We can feel insecure about pretty much anything, but some common insecurities are our body, our identity, our reputation, what God thinks, and what people think.

If we don't know or receive the truth, then we will be trapped in an endless cycle of insecurity and will look for acceptance and validation from people. The issue is that we live in a world where we can always find someone to validate a mindset. Just because a mindset, belief, or perspective is validated, does not mean it is right. People will search for validation because we love the feeling of synergy, community, and unity. But we and the person validating us can BOTH be wrong even in the validation. Truth is truth, regardless of what other people think. While we can always find someone in the world to validate us, we can also always find someone to criticize and attack us. It doesn't matter where we look or whom we ask, we can always find opposing opinions. In a world where everyone has a different opinion, how can you know what is right or wrong?

One of my favorite stories to illustrate this is the tale of a man and his son who went to the market with their donkey. To prepare for the market, the man put his son on the donkey and headed down the road. While they were walking, a neighbor saw them passing by and shouted, "Why are you letting your boy ride while you walk? Surely you should be on the donkey, and your son should walk." The man pulled his son off the donkey and got on instead. They went down the road a little further, and another man saw them. This man commented, "Why are you riding that poor donkey? Surely you can walk and not force your animal to carry all your weight." The man took a minute to think about it, and then quickly got off the donkey. They walked a little further, only to have yet another person comment on their situation. This third person told the man, "Why are you making the poor boy walk? Surely your donkey could carry him."

This is a wonderful story and actually helped me greatly in my journey of becoming secure in myself. There are an endless number of opinions that we can find if we look to people for our validation. We can be wrong and find someone who will validate us, and we can be right and find someone who will criticize us. The bottom line is that truth is truth, regardless of what people think. This is why the only way to have true peace and security is to agree with what Yahweh says. Yahweh is all-knowing, the author and finisher, the beginning and the end. He IS the way, the TRUTH, and the life. Who else would better know WHO we are and what are the right things to do?

The journey of becoming free from insecurity is simply a matter of discovering what Yahweh says and then choosing to agree with that truth regardless of what we think or were told. Remember that truth supersedes facts. Culture doesn't define us, Heaven does. What may be a subjective fact in your culture, may not be true in Heaven's eyes. Cultures, people, opinions, and perspectives come and go. Heaven's view is pure, and eternal, and goes beyond people's soul wounds and filters.

SHAME

While shame is not thought of as an insecurity, by definition it is just another form of feeling vulnerable, weak, and uncertain about an area of our life. Shame, just like every other lie, comes from the enemy, and it will kill, steal, and destroy our life as long as we are partnering with it. Religion loves to define us by our actions and our past. Religion never forgets, and worse yet, holds us in torment while shaming us for the things that Jesus has already forgotten...

> *Hebrews 8:12 (TPT) "For I will demonstrate my mercy to them and will forgive their evil deeds, and <u>never remember again their sins.</u>" [Emphasis mine]*

> *1 Peter 4:8b(ESV) "...love covers a multitude of sins."*

> *Romans 8:1 (TPT) "So now the case is closed. <u>There remains no accusing voice of condemnation</u> against those who are joined in life-union with Jesus, the Anointed One." [Emphasis mine]*

It is clear in scripture that God does NOT hold our sin over our heads and condemn us. SHAME defines us by our actions and by our past, but Yahweh defines us as blameless and by who we are in Jesus. As intense and hard as it is to face shame, it really boils down to this... one voice is the voice of TRUTH and LIFE, and the other is the voice of LIES and DEATH.

There is NOTHING good that comes from shame. I have heard people argue that shame and remembering the past helps them not repeat it. But partnering and agreeing with the lies of shame only perpetuates death and torment in our souls. When we define ourselves by something OTHER than what Jesus has said, then we either think we know better than Jesus, OR it reveals an area that we have bought into the lies of shame.

Facing shame can be very painful because again, shame has... FACTS. As we have learned, TRUTH supersedes FACTS, so it comes down to our choice yet again to decide which voice we are going to agree with. Shame is a liar... even though shame has facts to back up its accusations against us. Shame is the enemy, and we can choose to stop agreeing with its lies anymore. In fact, Jesus is eagerly waiting for us to agree with Him and choose freedom and life in place of shame.

BECOMING FREE & SECURE

I was at a conference years ago that was for college students who wanted more of Jesus. The conference was held in a huge indoor auditorium, and thousands of people were there. Our group sat in the front row, eager to see what God had in store for us. As the worship began, everyone stayed in their seats. People were singing and lifting their hands, but no one went up front to worship. While I was worshiping, Yahweh asked me to go up front and DANCE with Him. A million thoughts instantly ran through my mind... *What will people think? I will be the only one in front of thousands of people... dancing on top of it. It will look like I'm trying to "be spiritual" and get people to look at me. Why is Jesus asking me to do this? I can worship just as well right here in my seat...* But the invitation weighed heavy on me. Jesus has my "yes" no matter the cost. In my heart, I was only trying to obey the Lord, so that's all that mattered. I went up, in front of everyone, into the 20-foot gap between the chairs and the stage. I was all by myself and worshiped the whole time. It was SO uncomfortable. I didn't actually get to enjoy worship because I was so uncomfortable being upfront. Finally, worship ended, and I sat down.

Later that day, they did another round of worship for the evening session... and again, Yahweh asked me to come up and worship. This time was a little easier, but not much. It was still incredibly uncomfortable. During the first song, some of my friends came up and joined me. It was nice to not be alone up there, but I also was concerned that now we looked like we were trying to "be spiritual" and get people to look at us. But again, I reminded myself that Jesus has my "yes", and my motives were out of obedience. We stayed and worshiped the whole time, and again I was relieved when worship was done so I could go sit down.

The next day there was a shift. During the morning worship time, Yahweh asked me again to go up front to worship. I obeyed again and went up by myself, but this time, a couple of hundred other college students followed me and came up front! A movement had started. For the evening worship session, thousands of college students crammed up front to worship, filling up the isles. I was stunned. From no one going up front to it being packed was impressive to me. On that last night, while I was shoulder to shoulder with people worshipping up front, Yahweh thanked me for my obedience to come up alone and worship. He told me that I was a pioneer and that I plow the way for others to follow. All of my discomforts were worth it. If my sacrifice of worship helped others go deeper in their relationship and worship with Yahweh, then it was worth it.

When facing insecurity, sometimes it comes down to making the decision to obey in spite of the thoughts of insecurity in our heads. We are continually at a crossroads of choosing Yahweh's abundant life or the enemy's lies and fears. Beyond the facts... beyond what people have told us... beyond our experiences and our feelings, will we choose Jesus?

The bottom line is that as long as we are agreeing with lies, the enemy will always make sure there is something for us to be insecure or ashamed about. There are an infinite number of ways that they can suggest we are falling short. "*You should be more compassionate, patient, evangelical, prophetic, mystical, courageous, strong, flexible, pray longer, spend more time with family*" and on and on the list goes. The enemy is bloodthirsty and can never be appeased... ever. Any time we are agreeing with the enemy, it is endless torment for our soul. The freer we become, the more clearly we can see the lies and torment we were under.

As we deal with insecurity specifically, it is wonderful to be free from the weight of man's ever-changing opinions.

Yahweh's thoughts are constant towards us. He is not shaming, condemning, manipulating, controlling, or withholding. It is a wonderful new way to live as we begin to live on HIS word alone.

The process for facing our insecurities and shame looks the same as it does facing other soul wounds and lies:

4. Identify the insecurity or thing you feel shame about.

    o   Jesus, what is a lie that I am believing about myself or something I feel ashamed about that You would like to heal right now?

5. Break agreement with the lie or soul wound.

    o   Decide to not agree with and believe the lie. Verbally saying it out loud is very helpful.

6. Receive the truth Jesus shows you in place of the lie.

    o   What is the truth for me to stand on in place of the lies I was believing?

The journey of becoming secure is the same as any other soul transformation. It is not usually a one-and-done healing. Our soul has spent years clinging to the words of what people have said about us and the lies from the enemy. We can have a powerful encounter with Jesus that instantly heals our soul wounds, but usually our healing moves at the pace of our soul's capacity.

As we become more and more secure, we grow to be at rest within ourselves and in the way we view the world. The longer I have walked in agreement with Yahweh, the more confidence I have in Him. More and more, I know that all things are going to work out for GOOD. I know that even if it doesn't make sense, Yahweh's ways always bring LIFE. Everything He asks of me and everything He tells me is always for GOOD. Over time we will grow more and more confident in what Yahweh says about us and be able to reject the lies of the enemy easier and easier.

Insecure To Secure

Self-Application

KEYS TO REMEMBER

- Any area that we feel insecure, reveals an area of our heart that is not confident in and agreeing with what Yahweh says about us.

- Cultures, people, opinions, and perspectives come and go, but Heaven's view is pure, eternal, and goes beyond people's soul wounds and filters.

- Shame holds our past over us, but Yahweh chooses to forget our sin and to define us by our identity in Jesus.

- Like other soul healing, it comes down to our choice to believe what Yahweh says above anything else.

QUESTIONS TO ASK JESUS

- What insecurities do I have that you would like to talk about?

- What do you say about this insecurity?

- What truth is needed to displace the lies of insecurity that I have agreed with?

Remember each of these questions can be used as a springboard to identify lies, break agreement with them, and receive Jesus' truth instead. Please also reference Chapters 5 & 6 of The Foundation for help and troubleshooting blocks when trying to talk to Jesus about fear.

Chapter Eight

#TRIGGERED

Offense is a hot topic currently in western culture. Everyone seems to be deeply offended over something. Being "triggered" is a common phrase now. The problem is that when we don't bring our offenses to Jesus, we harden our hearts. This hardness and anger then become a block in our healing and stunt our soul's growth in Christ. As we have been talking about, to be healthy in our soul, it comes down to bringing everything to Jesus. When we bring Him our offense, we find healing and see a little more from Jesus's perspective.

Offense can come from our justice heart or from a soul wound that got poked by someone. Offense over injustice can harden our hearts, but it can also be the driving force that compels us to act against the injustice. We see examples of offense over injustice today in the "woke" culture. The woke culture says that it fights for social justice, and it seems to be offended by almost everything. In Chapter 5 of this book, *The Gift of Forgiveness*, I address the justice heart. Justice is a godly trait, and it is integral to the Kingdom. However, our judgment of justice is often misguided and flawed. Currently, we see examples of this regularly in the news. People who have bought into the "woke" ideology are misguided, but they genuinely believe what they think is true. From their perspective on abortion, gender dysphoria, economic issues, climate control, and so on, they are FULLY convinced that they have woken up to the "truth". And they are desperately trying to do the "right" thing. They are driven by offense and their desire for "justice".

We may not be acting out physically in response to our offenses (like the woke revolution we see today), but hear me clearly...

we are often JUST as misguided when we are offended. This is why it is so important to bring everything to Jesus. Our offense *could* be from a righteous anger, or we could be from a soulish place. The only way to truly know is if we bring it to Jesus. Often times there will be a mixture of soulish perspective and righteous anger. Like with everything else, the key is abiding IN Jesus.

> *Ephesians 4:26-27 (ESV) "Be angry and do not sin; do not let the sun go down on your anger, and give no opportunity to the devil."*

> *Psalm 4:4 (BSB) "Be angry, yet do not sin; on your bed, search your heart and be still. Selah"*

> *James 1:20 (NLT) "Human anger does not produce the righteousness God desires."*

Notice that these verses don't condemn anger. It is possible to have a righteous anger against the enemy. As we grow in sonship, our soul's perspective will continue to change drastically. We will shift more and more away from human anger and offense, and we will begin to think and see more as Yahweh does. There is a righteous anger and a righteous justice, but it looks vastly different from the human versions.

All in all, offense clouds our thinking, especially when the offense is rooted in a soul wound. Offense either comes from a justice heart, OR it is from a soulish reaction to an insecurity or soul wound. If someone pokes at a physical wound, the natural reaction would be to pull back and be angry at them. A very similar thing happens internally when we get offended. When our soul has a wound, the enemy can see it clearly and works to poke at it through the brokenness of other people. The person may not have even meant for the comment or action to be taken offensively, but because our soul is blinded by pain, we react as if it were an attack. Usually, we don't realize or understand that it was actually a preexisting soul wound that got poked. Then we shut down, angry and hurt that our wound was triggered.

Unaddressed offenses (both from perceived injustice and soul wounds) cause us to harden our hearts. The bigger the hurt and confusion on a subject, the bigger the offense. This hardening is what keeps our hearts stunted. The way out of offense is to bring it to Jesus.

One day I was dealing with offense and unforgiveness toward someone. I went to talk to Jesus about it because I wanted Jesus more than I wanted to hold on to my anger and offense. When I went on the encounter, what I saw shocked me! I saw myself holding poop in my hands. I was CHOOSING to hold onto this nasty, stinky poop. I was obsessed and fixated on holding it, and I was completely blind to see what it really was. When Jesus offered to take the poop, I pulled away from Him and clung to the poop more tightly, which made it squish in between my fingers and get on my clothes. Thankfully, when I pulled away from Jesus, and it got all over me... the blinders were taken off. I could see it for what it was, and I smelled the stink that anger and offense were causing. I was shocked and slightly embarrassed that I couldn't see it before. I quickly turned back to Jesus who still had His hands out, waiting to help me. I gave Him the poop, and He was GLAD to take it. He wasn't grossed out or offended. He seemed relieved that I had come to my senses. Jesus wiped my hands clean and gave me new clothes in exchange for the poop-covered ones. The poop was OBVIOUSLY gross and nasty. But I was so blinded by offense and unforgiveness that I couldn't see it for what it really was. This blindness happens to us every day when we allow our soul wounds to remain in our hearts.

Instead of shutting down, we can view every offense as an invitation to freedom. Every time we get offended, it is HIGHLIGHTING an area of our heart that can be healed, or it is pointing out a place where our justice heart can grow in sonship. Instead of partnering with an offense, we can use the offense as a springboard to bring us more breakthroughs and revelation!

Now, this sounds nice. It is a wonderful idea to turn our offense into something that brings healing. But walking it out can be

QUITE hard. When we have a wound, physically or emotionally, our natural response is to self-protect. When we are angry and hurt because someone offended us, the last thing we want to do is deal with the offense! Our flesh wants to simmer in the hurtful event until justice is served, but the simmering only adds more pain.

Offense stands in the way of our healing. To be free of offense, there are a few things to understand and do:

- Forgiveness is the first step to healing and freedom. As long as we harbor offense against someone or an event, we are stuck. So, choosing to release the offense and surrender it to Jesus is where to start.

- Once we have released the offense to Jesus, then it helps to allow Him to speak to us about that area of our heart. He may reveal an insecurity in our heart that caused the offense, OR He may elevate our justice heart to view things through Heaven's eyes.

- Lastly, the choice before us is to choose Jesus or go back to the offense. Whatever Jesus showed you about the offense is your way to freedom. Remember that He is the Way, the Truth, and the Life. So anytime Jesus shows you the truth, it is an invitation to LIFE and to see more from Heaven's perspective.

UNOFFENDABLE

The more we bring our offenses to Jesus, the more we will become unoffendable. As our soul heals and matures, our heart grows more sensitive towards Yahweh. We also will begin to see the broken souls BEHIND people's actions. It is possible to be unoffendable and maintain a Heavenly perspective as our heart shifts from being offended to having compassion for people's brokenness. The more we fix our eyes on Jesus, the more we will view life through the eyes of love. Like everything else for our soul, it takes time to become unoffendable, but it is possible.

I have successfully been able to remain unoffended during some arguments with my husband. It sounds funny to even mention it, but our spouses can offend us more than anyone! So, the first time I was able to be at rest and unoffended during a disagreement, it was a true sign of being able to live unoffendable! No matter the circumstance or offender, it is possible for us to see everyone and everything through the eyes of Love. We are seated in Heavenly places, one with Jesus Himself, and HE empowers us to do the impossible.

When a circumstance or person steals our peace, it is because WE let them. There is no condemnation if we do become offended or forget to walk in our identity. To reset, we can bring the offense to Jesus and ask Him to show us how the offense snuck in and how to get it out. The more we prioritize staying in peace and walking in our identity, the more unshakeable we will become.

#Triggered

Self-Application

KEYS TO REMEMBER

- Offense comes from two different places: an angry reaction to a soul wound that got poked or from a justice heart.

- Offense causes a hardened heart which leads to stunting our growth and puts resistance in our soul when we engage with God.

- Just because our offense can be validated by an injustice or soul wound, that doesn't justify our partnership with an offense as sons of God.

- We can live unoffendable and unshakable regardless of our circumstances.

QUESTIONS TO ASK JESUS

- What or who has offended me that You would like to talk to me about? How do YOU view the situation? What is the truth?

- How do I get free from the things I am offended over in my heart?

- What does it look like to be unoffendable? How do I grow to be unoffendable?

Remember each of these questions can be used as a springboard to identify lies, break agreement with them, and receive Jesus' truth instead. Please also reference Chapters 5 & 6 of The Foundation for help and troubleshooting blocks when trying to talk to Jesus about fear.

Chapter Nine

OVERCOMING EXHAUSTION

In 2011, I had a full psychological breakdown. Crazy person, staring at the wall, unable to do basic things level of breakdown. My husband now, then boyfriend, cared for me during this time. He made me food and sat with me in my darkness. To try to help me recover, he asked me to brush my hair... and the stress of that simple task sent me into tears of distress. I felt lost in a dark void, and I didn't know how to get out. I knew God was with me and that I was one with Him, but I couldn't feel Him at all. I spent hours each day staring at the wall... or ceiling... waiting to feel something other than my despair. I took a little comfort in knowing that God was there with me, but I wished He would make His presence known to me. I knew it was my issue and that Yahweh was indeed speaking to me. I was just too shut down to hear it. My adrenal glands were shot, and my body was worn thin. Physically and emotionally, I was spent. When you are already tired, it is exhausting to try to pull yourself out. When you have nothing left to give, how can you give it all to Jesus?

It took me a long time to heal from the mess I was in. It was a slow progression, but eventually, I did heal. I really prefer to just sort things out and *"git 'er done"* fast, but that was NOT the case with healing from my breakdown. I was broken in my soul and body, and both took a long time to recover. My soul was so shut down and exhausted that it took a couple of weeks before I could do basic life again. And it took months before I was able to hear Jesus again. (I want to point out again that Jesus was always talking to me, I was just too shut down to hear Him. He did not abandon me in my darkest moments.) As for my body, it took close to 2 years for my adrenal glands to recover. I believed for instant healing in my body and soul, but in this case, it took lots of vitamins, naps, and saying "no" to events for my body to recover. It was NOT a fun process, especially for someone who likes to get things done fast. But I did heal. Jesus was big enough.

There is a promise that we are given for hard times. Yahweh promises that there will always be enough... that His grace is sufficient for us. I was haunted by this verse for years. *Why wasn't God enough for my breakdown? Why didn't He come in and save me?* It took years before these questions were answered. Oddly enough, my answer to these questions came during my miscarriage. After losing my baby, I was desperate to be close to Jesus. There was such a deep level of surrender in that season because I was determined to not give the enemy any real estate in my heart. I refused to let losing my son become a foothold of fear and pain in my life. I unknowingly harbored the questions and accusations against God regarding my breakdown for 6 years. Because of my desperation to not have anything between me and Yahweh during my miscarriage, I finally laid those accusations down on my altar in Heaven. And of all things, that area of my heart was the first to be healed during the miscarriage...

I went on an encounter, and I immediately laid everything on the altar. *[See Chapter 3 of Growing in Sonship (Book 2) for surrendering reference]* Everything I understood and could express... and even the things I couldn't put words to or explain were laid down. I was desperate to be as close to Jesus as possible during my deep pain. I knew that anything that I held back would be an area where I would pull away from Jesus. So, I diligently tried to lay it all down... my son whom I lost, my pain, my questions, my accusations against God, my fears, my past, my future, EVERYTHING. After I laid it all down, I intentionally walked AWAY from all the deep pain and emotion, and I turned my face towards Jesus. He was sitting down beside a brook near the altar, so I went and sat with Him. Just sitting in His presence was healing without even having to say a word. After a while, Jesus turned to me and asked, "Jessica, would you like to know why My grace wasn't enough for you when you had your breakdown?" I was shocked! After all these years, FINALLY, I got to have my answer! With attitude, I replied back, "Yes, I WOULD like to know why you weren't enough for that season!" Jesus kindly...and gently continued, "This is the first time that you have released the accusation against Me in that area, so now we can finally talk about it. Now that you have surrendered it, I can answer the questions that have haunted you all these years." Jesus paused. I knew whatever He was going to say next was going to be big. I waited in anticipation, and then He continued, "Jessica, the reason why you broke was because you agreed with the lie 'I can't do this.' If you had continually agreed with TRUTH, *that My grace is sufficient for you*, then you wouldn't have had the breakdown."

There it was. It was like a bomb went off in my head. All the accusations and anger that I harbored against God were obliterated. When Jesus spoke truth over me, TRUTH took the blinders off my eyes. I saw/remembered the months leading up to the breakdown. It was like a timeline rolled out, and I could see the slow progression that I took as I agreed with the lie "I can't do this." I was tired and not taking care of my body. I was burning the candle at both ends when I heard just whispers of lies that said, "I'm tired." "This is too much for me." And then the lies grew to "I can't do this." I took the bait, and I partnered with these LIES. Whenever we agree with a lie, we give it authority and power over our life. I agreed with the lies, first in my thoughts. Then, I began to speak those lies to my co-workers and friends. As the months went on, the lie was growing in strength over my life. I blindly fed this ravenous beast that wanted to steal, kill, and destroy my life. And it could have done just that if I had chosen to harden my heart against Jesus instead of turning towards Him. Because I chose Jesus over the accusation and questions, I found healing and revelation... that the breakdown was my doing.

What we behold, we become. Likewise, what we agree with, we submit to and give power over our life. This is why it is such a big deal for sons of God to renew their minds. The more lies we agree with, the more death we partner with in our souls. Believers continually are blind-sided by our agreement with lies and then blame Jesus for "not showing up".

If I had agreed with TRUTH and stood firm that His grace was enough for me, I am convinced that I wouldn't have had a full-on breakdown. God's promises are available to us, but it is still our choice to agree with them. Our choice to agree with truth or lies determines our healing, health, and future.

OVERCOMING

From my observations, exhaustion comes from two things: agreeing with the lies of the enemy AND a lack of boundaries which spreads us too thin. Either of these roots can cause exhaustion, but almost always you will find both of these factors at play when someone is feeling exhausted. The prevention of exhaustion AND the way out of exhaustion both require us to be intentional in two areas: boundaries and our thoughts.

In Chapter 8 of *Growing in Sonship* (Book 2 of this series), I discuss boundaries in depth. In summary, healthy boundaries create an internal standard with checks and balances to maintain our inner peace. Self-checks are simply being aware and intentional with how our inner world is doing. If anything is out-of-whack, then we bring it to Jesus. When we have healthy boundaries, it is us choosing Jesus and His peace over anything else. If we cave to the pressure of the "should", "have to", or manipulation from people, then we are using our free will to partner with something other than Jesus' rest. Jesus doesn't do things because He *should*. He is a KING, and kings do things intentionally and powerfully. When the Father led Jesus to heal the sick, then Jesus healed the sick. And when the Father led Jesus to take a nap or to withdraw from the crowd (ministry), then Jesus followed. Jesus ONLY did what He saw the Father doing. He said "no" to things, NOT to reject people, but out of obedience to His Father. Giving our "yes" to Jesus requires us to say "no" to other things. That is our example of healthy boundaries.

When we don't choose healthy boundaries, it opens the door for *should* and *manipulation* to drain the life out of us. Any area that we are not in agreement with truth is an area that sucks the life out of us... which makes us EXHAUSTED. Healthy boundaries keep us healthy and at rest, which protects us from exhaustion on a physical and emotional level. Healthy people have healthy boundaries as we saw in Jesus' life.

The other cause for exhaustion is partnering with lies like: "*I can't do this*", "*This is too hard for me*", or "*I am tired or exhausted.*" These types of statements are lies because none of these are true for Jesus. In Jesus, all these are possible (Philippians 4:13) so "*I can't do this*" or "*This is too hard for me*" are lies. Besides, Jesus is not tired or exhausted. His grace is sufficient, and He carries our burden, so our yoke is easy. We can agree with the promises of God and pull the power of those verses into our reality... OR we can agree with the lies of the enemy and give power to the lies to steal, kill, and destroy our reality.

In my journey of healing, I didn't realize until years later that I had given power and authority to the lies and that THEY were the ones who broke me. My soul was so shut down that I couldn't see or hear anything that Jesus was saying during my breakdown. At that point in my walk with the Lord, I knew that He would never leave me, that He was always talking to me, and that He was pursuing me and my healing. However, going on encounters "*didn't work*" because my soul was too tired (from believing lies) to be able to connect to Jesus. I knew my soul was so broken and shut down that it didn't have the capacity to engage with Yahweh at all. So instead, I chose to turn my heart and intention towards Him continually even though I *felt* nothing. I regularly said out loud things like, "I know You will never leave me or forsake me", "Thank you for being big enough for everything I face", "I know you are speaking right now", and "It's just You and me Jesus. I will always choose You." I tried hard to not focus on questions and accusations against the Lord because I knew those would only stunt (and possibly even prevent) my healing and recovery.

As I meditated on the truth, things slowly shifted in my soul, and I began to recover from my breakdown. I discuss meditation in depth in Chapter 4 of The Foundation (Book 1). I describe meditation as marination. For example, focusing on our pain, exhaustion, and hopelessness only marinates our soul in negative and despairing things. What we fixate on and spend our emotional energy thinking about creates and reveals our belief system. The key to healthy meditation is to bring the pain, exhaustion, hopelessness, and frankly EVERYTHING, to Jesus and then choose to focus on TRUTH instead. This is VERY different from deflection or distracting yourself from the negative and despairing areas of your soul.

Deflection is simply ignoring the elephant in the room (distracting yourself from thinking about it) while leaving your soul in a place of being crushed by its weight. What I am talking about is acknowledging the elephant, bringing it to Jesus (surrender), and then choosing to focus on Jesus and His truth instead of the elephant. Deflection ignores the elephant; surrender is giving the elephant to Jesus because you are choosing HIM over everything else. Even if you *feel* so shut down that you can't connect or *feel* Jesus (like I was), you can still choose to surrender the elephant and meditate on truth.

Of course, if you are in a place where you can still connect, even in a small way, then going on an encounter and talking to Jesus will quicken your soul's recovery from exhaustion. Having healthy boundaries and being diligent in our thoughts are important parts of overcoming and/or preventing exhaustion but engaging with Jesus is vital... HE is the healer! In reality, keeping our eyes fixed on Jesus is the least tiring way to overcome exhaustion. Overcoming exhaustion is challenging because our soul is already at the point of burnout. To be victorious requires us to dig deep and stand firm on truth. Even in our exhaustion, it is possible to be healed and fully recover because Jesus is empowering us!

I am confident that we can be fully healed instantaneously. I have faith for instant healings and have seen them happen for other people. But usually, our soul is too tired to receive or believe for total healing when we are at the point of exhaustion. Having healthy boundaries, watching our thoughts, and of course, connecting with Jesus are key; but there are things we can do to help support our recovery from exhaustion on a practical level. These things are only for SUPPORT; they themselves cannot heal you. Jesus is the only way, the truth, and the life for our soul and for overcoming exhaustion. A cast supports an injury which helps it heal faster, but it is not the healer itself. The list below are things that support our soul while it is healing, but they are not the healing element. These are the things that helped me recover...

- Be PATIENT with yourself and your healing.

  o Being frustrated or discouraged with your progress will only slow your healing. Frustration and discouragement are not Heavenly concepts, so to partner with them brings death to our souls. As hard as it may be, it is very helpful to be patient and gracious with yourself as you heal and grow. And that doesn't just go for recovering from exhaustion. This goes for EVERY area of our life.

- Self-check: intentionally being self-aware of feelings and triggers. Why do I feel exhausted? Is it a person, work, or past event that I am still carrying? What feels hopeless in my life?

  o Once you have identified those things, then you can bring them to Jesus and see what HE says about them. Ask Jesus why those things are affecting you, and what needs to be done so you aren't affected by them.

- Supplements: vitamins and/or minerals.

  o If we don't receive instant healing, then supporting our body during recovery can be very helpful. I found making a greens powder, spirulina, and maca powder smoothie helped. Giving extra nutrients to my body whether through supplements or juicing helped my body heal. For supplements, I took ashwagandha, a multivitamin, and a mineral supplement because my body was so depleted.

- Avoid drinking or taking any form of caffeine.

  o I think we have become dependent on caffeine to function because our bodies are not supported with enough rest and nutrition. I loved my coffee and energy drinks. I lived off them. But during my breakdown, I realized that I was FORCING my adrenal glands and body to function when they really needed to rest and heal. Caffeine in reality is a drug, and it is addicting. When recovering from my breakdown, I cut out all caffeinated supplements and drinks. Once I was healed and still to this day, I only drink caffeine on special occasions because I am trying to be kind to my body and adrenals.

- Say "no" to things.

  o Everything I say "yes" to, requires energy and effort. I began to be very guarded about what I chose to do with my free time. As much as I wanted to go hang out with friends, I would stay home instead if I knew it would cost a lot of energy on my body or soul. It was hard to learn to be free of the torments of *Should*, but it was very rewarding because I began to be less and less exhausted.

The list above helped support my healing, but the actual healing came from Jesus as I meditated on truth and chose boundaries that protected my rest and inner peace. My healing was not instant. It was a long, slow recovery for me emotionally and physically. (I was so broken and shut down that just the idea of brushing my hair overwhelmed me to the point of tears...) So, if you are in the midst of a psychological breakdown, then there is hope for you and for making a FULL recovery. And if you are not to that level of exhaustion and desperation, then your healing can be faster than mine was.

Bottom line, there is hope, and you can be healed. Jesus is big enough for everything you face, and exhaustion is not your destination or God's plan for your life. It will take patience and diligence, which seems all the more exhausting when you are already tired... but the Truth will set you free. As you align yourself with Truth, He will heal and restore your life. You can be whole. Exhaustion is not your inheritance.

Overcoming Exhaustion

Self-Application

KEYS TO REMEMBER

- Whenever we agree with a lie (like "I can't do this" or "I'm overwhelmed"), we give it authority and power over our life.

- Exhaustion affects our soul and physical body, therefore, healing and recovering from exhaustion is a multi-dimensional process.

- Recovering from exhaustion begins as we choose to have healthy boundaries and are diligent to agree with/ meditate on truth.

- There are other things we can do to support our healing and recovery from exhaustion, but those things only support healing. Jesus is the only Healer.

QUESTIONS TO ASK JESUS

- What do You want to tell me about the areas of my life where I feel exhausted?

- What is the root of my exhaustion?

- How do I heal and recover this area of my life?

- What do I need to know or do to prevent exhaustion in the future?

Remember each of these questions can be used as a springboard to identify lies, break agreement with them, and receive Jesus' truth instead. Please also reference Chapters 5 & 6 of The Foundation for help and troubleshooting blocks when trying to talk to Jesus about fear.

Chapter Ten

WALKING OUT WHOLENESS

To "crush it" or to be crushed... the choice is yours!

We didn't cover every soul wound in this book, but we did discuss a lot of them. Even with all the information shared, it is still vital to actually bring your soul wounds, grief, and offenses to Jesus. This book will only become more head knowledge if you do not allow JESUS to show your soul the truth in what was said. I define head knowledge as anything you have learned *about* Jesus but don't truly know or believe in your heart (soul). I can read a biography *about* someone, but I don't truly *know* them unless I have a personal relationship with them. Our soul cannot and will not be healed through head knowledge. Third-dimensional teachings and even revelation will always fall short of healing our fourth-dimensional soul until we receive spirit-to-spirit revelation from Jesus.

> Revelation 3:20 *"I stand at the door and knock, anyone who hears my voice AND opens the door. I will come in and have* <u>deep and blissful intimacy</u> *with him and He with me." (Translation by the author — explained in Ch. 3 of The Foundation)*

Ian Clayton estimates that all believers have between 7-9 familiar lies that we agree with and are totally blind to. A familiar lie is a generational lie that has been in your family so long that it feels *familiar* or just a part of "who you are". If you were born with earplugs in your ears, then the feeling of them in your ears and the world being much quieter would be NORMAL to you. It's all that you have known. The same thing happens with familiar lies.

Let's say your entire family is controlling. Control would be the system that you know how to operate from. Until our hearts soften and are ready to receive from Jesus in the blind areas of our souls, we have no grid for any other way of living.

This was the case for me when dealing with a poverty spirit. Agreeing with the lies of poverty ran deep in my family line. It was all that I knew, and I was completely and totally blind to it. One day, Yahweh told me I couldn't grow anymore in my faith until I dealt with my agreement with poverty. He explained that poverty was stunting my growth. I knew I was totally blind to poverty, so I started off the encounter by asking Jesus to show me what poverty looked like in the spirit. (*It helps me personally to see the nasty lies so it sinks into my heart that they ARE actually the enemy and bring death into my life.*) I was shocked to see a leathery-skinned creature with human-ish features. Its skin clung to its bones, and as I studied it, I realized that its body was actually impoverished. I thanked Jesus for showing me what it looked like, but I was still totally blind to his lies. I then asked Jesus to show me some of the lies that poverty was saying. I saw the creature say a few phrases, "There's not enough...I need to save...I have to work for money." Each phrase came out from the mouth of poverty, like a green stinky fart vapor you would see in a kid's movie. And as each green vapor left his mouth, I watched myself addictively breathe it in with a deep inhale. Like a good hit, my soul drank in the words of poverty. When I saw the vision, I was totally disgusted. It was a major wake-up call to my soul. But I still didn't know the way out. Those phrases that poverty said *felt* true. They were all that I knew. Then I asked Jesus, "What is the truth? What do you say about this?" I was expecting to hear something like, "*There is always enough.*" That kind of an answer felt trivial and shallow to my entrenched soul... but of course, Jesus rose above my expectations. He gently explained, "Poverty is the enemy, but you have to decide that for yourself. HE is the one who is stealing your finances and bringing death to your life. He hates you and wants to see your destruction."

I was so confused. I knew what Jesus said was true... but it didn't *feel* true. I felt that poverty had helped me be a "saver" which I thought protected my finances. Furthermore, I had always had enough for every bill, so how was poverty stealing from me? We may not have had much left over, but every bill had always been covered... which I credited Jesus. So, it didn't make sense when Jesus said poverty was robbing our finances. I remembered years before when I dealt with shame in my life. The lies of shame felt true... until I got free. It wasn't until I aligned with truth, that my mind became sound, and I could see the lies. I decided to agree again with what Jesus said... even though it didn't make sense. I chose to believe that my poverty mentality was NOT a protector or helper but rather MY enemy. I declared and divorced my agreements with the enemy and chose to receive what Jesus said. *(Divorce was the word that came to mind in the encounter because I was SO tightly bound to poverty. It was like I needed to divorce my vow and allegiance to poverty.)*

Life went on after the encounter, but things began to change. Within a few weeks, someone gave us a ten-thousand-dollar check. Then the next month, we were given another two thousand dollars. I was floored! We had always just had enough. We scraped by but were thankful that at least each bill was able to be paid. I asked Yahweh about it, and He said, "THIS is abundance. Poverty was robbing your finances and just making ends meet."

After that, money didn't keep coming in large sums, but that encounter and what happened has stayed with me. My husband and I are still exploring how to live from the financing of Heaven. We have hit hard times financially, even recently, but we refuse to allow circumstances to change our belief system. Yahweh and His truth define our life, not our circumstances. When we don't see the promises of God manifest in our lives, we still choose Jesus and fix our eyes on Him. He is all we need, and He has our "yes" no matter the circumstance.

I shared that story to give an example of what to do with lies that we are totally blind to. If Jesus has highlighted an area of your life that is a familiar lie to you, then here are some steps that can help you get free from it...

1. Ask Yahweh to show you what the lying spirit looks like to help you recognize that it IS the enemy. When you see the chains, the nasty-looking demon, or however else it manifests in the encounter, it can help shake you out of the desire to partner with the lie.

2. Once you see it for what it is, ask Jesus, "What are the lies that this enemy is trying to sell me?"

3. After you can see the enemy and hear its lies, ask Jesus what HE says about it. It is important to hear the truth from Jesus. Even if it doesn't sound true at the moment, HIS words are the words of life.

4. Lastly, choose to break agreement with the enemy. No matter how true the lies sound, decide that the lies... are lies. And intentionally choose to receive and stand on what Jesus says in its place.

There are lies that are recognizable to us, and then there are lies and soul wounds that we are totally blind to. The steps above can help us see and break free from the lies and brokenness that we have carried all or most of our lives.

I want to be very clear that ANY emotion or thought we agree with that is not in Heaven WILL bring death even if it doesn't *feel* like it. Fear, control, anger, poverty, rejection, and any other lies ONLY have the capacity to bring us death. Even though the ONLY thing we get from the partnership is death, it will be disguised as a pseudo-benefit. For example, control uses us to bring death on the earth while only giving us a pseudo-peace (that everything will work out because we are in "control"). In reality, control is ONLY an illusion because we can't *control* ANYTHING. We can't control other people or our circumstances. Even our own bodies we have very limited *control* over (Hair color, how fast your nails grow, the changes your body makes over time, etc.)

Once I realized that there was no ability to appease the lies, with no ability to find peace through them, it didn't make sense to stay in the torment. I decided that I wanted to break free from the torment and choose Truth regardless of how Truth *felt* to my soul. Our enemy is never satisfied and will continually work to deceive us as long as we are choosing to agree with them. Here are a few of the common lies that we think we can appease and eventually find peace with...

- "I will be able to rest, once I get my to-do list done". *What we don't realize is that the list is eternally growing.*

- "I will feel beautiful if I just..." *Annnd the enemy makes sure to continually be changing the standard of beauty.*

- "I will be able to relax once I have this (amount) of money" *Sure, until you get there. Then you will decide it's not enough or that you have to keep striving to maintain and/or grow that money.*

- "I won't feel alone once I get married or find a friend" *Loneliness has nothing to do with your physical circumstances and everything to do with your soul's beliefs and wounds.*

- "My Christian "grade" and standing with God depends on my church attendance, service, and tithe" *There is no "grade." Our standing with God never changes. We were given the righteousness of Christ.*

The enemy will always make sure to move the goal... usually just out of reach so it *feels* attainable. As long as we are on the hook, we will be in never-ending torment. So, if it's not found in Heaven, let's not give them any real estate of our heart either.

Beyond realizing that I wanted off the hook, I also found a few other things that were helpful to me in my journey. I hope this list is helpful to you too...

- Celebrate each healing, encounter, and victory no matter how small it *feels*.

    o Don't despise the small beginnings. Our breakthroughs and healing happen at the pace of our soul's capacity and willingness to face the painful areas in our life. As I mentioned earlier, partnering with frustration and discouragement only stunts our growth. Instead, look for Yahweh in everything. I suggest you ask Him what HE thinks of the small healings and then agree with whatever He says.

- Receive every encounter as if everything Jesus says and does is intentional... because it is!

    o In the Bible, we see that God loves parables and symbolism. The same goes for what we sense in encounters! Many times, our soul will scoff at how "insignificant" a word or encounter felt. But if we push past those feelings, we can begin to unravel the depth, mystery, and power of what Jesus was revealing! It changes the position of our hearts from judgment to one of gratitude and receiving. Sometimes the smallest, most insignificant details can be the most precious ones. But all of that beauty and power is missed when we disregard encounters because they didn't meet our broken soul's expectations.

- Be kind, gracious, and patient with YOURSELF in the process

    o If self-criticism was helpful to our process, then we would see it in Jesus's life. We don't want our voice to oppose what Yahweh says and feels about us. Self-condemnation, self-criticism, and harshness do not and cannot help us in our journey. Though it may be challenging, learning to treat ourselves the same way Yahweh does, is very freeing and healing!

- Be self-aware

    o Personally, I like to set alarms on my phone to remind me to self-check. You find another way to remind yourself to check in with your heart; bottom line is to find some way to become self-aware. The more we pay attention to our inner world and test it against the truth, the faster we will heal and see breakthroughs. For example, as a child, I would mindlessly check out and daydream all day long. One day, Jesus showed me that my daydreaming was out of my dysfunction and pain. I never realized that I was checking out; it was just something I had always done. When Jesus pointed it out to me though, I was SHOCKED to see how my daydreams were rooted in fear and lies. My inner world was a mess, and I had layers of dysfunction that I never realized were there before! The more self-aware I became, the more breakthrough I saw as I brought everything to Jesus. I no longer felt the urge to check out. Instead, I would go engage with Jesus in a REAL encounter!

- Exercise your soul's capacity

    o Things like fasting, working out, or choosing to spend less time on TV or social media, are all examples of growing our soul's self-control. While these things probably don't directly correlate to our soul wounds, growing our self-discipline does help us in the healing journey. Saying no to our flesh, little by little, weakens our flesh, which makes it easier to say "YES!" to Jesus.

- Don't give up!

  - o Our soul needs just a moment with Jesus to be forever changed! In an instant, we can be permanently and radically transformed. As beautiful and precious as this is, it is not the norm. (And that is ok because the history we build with Jesus is worth more than anything!) Our souls have spent years entrenched in lies and wounds. This dysfunctional way of living is the habit and autopilot for our soul... which is why we usually have to bring things multiple times to Jesus. This repetition of bringing things to Jesus usually feels discouraging. It feels like "it's not working", but that is far from the case! EVERY single time we bring something to Jesus, it is a victory, it brings healing, and it retrains our soul. The key to know is that when our soul defaults into the old autopilot, it is not as strong as it was! Our soul may have reverted, but it is now at a lower percentage of the strength it was before. For example: 95%, then 90%, then 86%, etc. The soul's return to the old autopilot depends on the depth in which your soul receives the encounters and truth it was given. Two steps forward and one step back is still progress. It may feel slow and like "it's not working", but those are just discouraging thoughts from the enemy who is trying to keep you bound in torment. Don't be discouraged. Don't give up. Jesus IS big enough. And it IS working!

Years ago, Yahweh asked something odd of me. I had braces at the time, and I HATED flossing them. It took so long to thread under the wire of the braces, so I rarely did it. Then for some reason, Yahweh asked me to floss my teeth one night. I begrudgingly obeyed even though I saw NO kingdom value in it. Then the next night, He asked me again to floss. The pattern continued for a whole year! Each time I chose to obey, but it didn't get easier. My heart didn't shift, and I never settled into a happy routine. Every night that Yahweh asked me to floss, I obeyed but questioned how in the world this was doing anything for my soul healing or the kingdom. I obeyed because Yahweh has my "yes". After the year, Yahweh stopped asking me to floss every night. In fact, He hasn't asked me to floss since then! I thought maybe I would get a download, breakthrough, or healing when He stopped asking, but nothing came...

Years later, I was going through a hard time, but there was an anchoring in my soul that I hadn't experienced before. There was peace and revelation at the moment that I didn't know beforehand... at least I didn't know that I knew. After the revelation bubbled up out of me, I heard Jesus say to me, "This was deposited in you during your obedience in flossing." I don't know if I was more confused or in awe when He spoke. Flossing my teeth WAS doing something after all! Then I began to wonder, "Why flossing? How come I didn't see a shift or difference until now? How did my obedience to Yahweh translate into soul revelation and strength?" It was outside my box, and I thoroughly enjoyed that Jesus used foolish things to confound me.

I still don't have full revelation on what Jesus was doing in my heart during that time, but I wanted to share that story because our journey with Yahweh is unconventional. In this book, we discussed helpful tools, tips, and wisdom, but there will still be things that come out of the left field. The more we cling to Jesus, even if it doesn't make sense, the quicker we will heal and see a breakthrough.

I wanted to mention that I STILL use the tools and processes discussed in this book to conquer the lies my soul believes. The process and healing come quicker, but it still comes down to rejecting the lies and choosing what Jesus says instead. Even more simplified, our inner healing comes down to our ability to receive Truth. JESUS finished it. JESUS is our healer. JESUS bears our burdens. And JESUS is our strength. All we do is receive...Receive Jesus and His truth. Rely on His strength. Give our burdens to Him. Receive His healing. Once we agree with Jesus, the rest is done for us. It is finished.

> Revelation 3:20 "I stand at the door and knock, anyone who hears my voice AND opens the door. I will come in and have deep and blissful intimacy with him and He with me." (Translation by the author — explained in Ch. 3 of The Foundation)

> 1 John 2:24-25 (TPT) "So you must be sure to keep the message burning in your hearts; that is, the message of life you heard from the beginning. If you do, you will always be living in close fellowship with the Son and with the Father. And he himself has promised us the never-ending life of the ages to come!"

Ablaze

There is a flame that stands at the door
I hear His knock and whisper
The darkness in my soul shakes
He knows my name
But what about the pain?

Consuming fire consuming me
How wonderful yet terrible
All my fears come crashing in
But I am drawn to His whisper

As I open the door, I can see
That the darkness is not me
My fears are burning
My wounds are healing
My shame is fading
Refiner's fire refining me

I was afraid of the pain
But this fire is healing rain
The fire hurts, and yet it doesn't
It burns only if I resist
So I relent and give in
Consuming fire consuming me

The more I burn
The more I see
The more I feel
The more I hear
Refiner's fire refining me
Consuming fire consuming me

After a while, I can see
That the fire is now me
The flame that once brought fear
Is now my shalom
I am that which I used to fear
I became the fire
I am the fire
Ablaze for all eternity
Walking Out Wholeness

Self-Application

KEYS TO REMEMBER

- Our healing and breakthrough come down to our soul's choice to receive and stand on Jesus' truth as we encounter Him.

- The average believer has 7–9 familiar lies that we are totally blind to.

- Yahweh loves freeing us from our boxes and old systems. Embrace the odd things He asks of you. There's purpose in them.

QUESTIONS TO ASK JESUS

- What do You want to heal in my heart today?

    o   What lies am I believing about this area?

    o   What do YOU say about it?

    o   What truth do I need to cling to in place of the lies?

- Do I have any lies or soul wounds that I am totally blind to... and that I am ready to be free from?

- What do You want to teach or show me today?

- What's on Your heart?

SCRIPTURE PERMISSIONS

Scriptures are quoted from five main translations:

- ☐ Berean Study Bible (BSB)
- ☐ English Standard Version (ESV)
- ☐ New Living Translation (NLT)
- ☐ The Passion Translation (TPT)

Permissions are as follows:

ABOUT THE AUTHOR

Jessica Onsaga was a nobody from
nowhere who discovered she was a
son of God.

SeraphCreative

Heaven's Heart for Earth

Seraph Creative is a collective of artists, writers, theologians & illustrators who desire to see the body of Christ grow into full maturity, walking in their inheritance as Sons of God on the Earth.

Sign up to our newsletter to know about future exciting releases.

Visit our website :

www.seraphcreative.org